BORN ON THE FIFTH OF JULY:

Memoirs of Frontline Nurse, Captain Fred Phelps During The Bloodiest Years of Vietnam

By Fredrick O. Phelps

With Notes by Chris Kassel

With sincere best wishes to Joyce and Roger —

Fred

Foreword: The Colesburg Spirit

Paging through a historical perspective of Colesburg, Iowa (like the one published in 1993) gives you a pretty good idea of how a small town in the heart of Midwest America is supposed to work. Photos from the sixties, the fifties, the forties—even the thirties—show businesses that are still in operation; the captions lists surnames that are still prominent throughout Delaware County and Colony Township.

An article in the *Corn and Coffee Press*, the Colesburg Consolidated School's student newspaper, appeared in 1930 under the title 'The Colesburg Spirit'. In part, it read:

The spirit of the people of Colesburg is one of the most splendid, it seems to us, of any of them. It is one of cooperation, of helping one another, of being a friend to one in need.

In school we have a wonderful spirit; everyone is working together. 'All for one and one for all' seems to be the motto. Strangers coming in are welcomed by smiles and warm friendship on the part of everyone. They go away seemingly helped and strengthened by the thought of the fine attitude of the pupils and teachers, and they seem to know that they will be welcome the next time they come.

With such a spirit resting upon our town, we can feel lucky that we live here and should do our part to keep up Colesburg's reputation.

At first, this brand of bright-eyed optimism seems typical of America before the cynicism of modernity settled in, but then you recall that this was written in 1930—possibly the most desperate hours that this country has ever seen. Iowa farmers were among the earliest and hardest hit by the Great Depression; for them, the economic collapse began long before the Wall Street closing bells in October, 1929. Crop prices had been dropping throughout the twenties, and by the time that the death knell sounded in the last months of the decade, the cost of seed, fuel, labor, rent and taxes had already exceeded the income of the average Iowa farmer by 35%. Soon, that number rose to 50%.

The day the above missive, in all of its hope, humanity and simple optimism was published in the *Corn and Coffee Press,* corn was selling for eight cents a bushel, pork for three cents a pound, beef for five cents a pound and you could pick up a dozen eggs for a dime. And, of course, there was no reduction in the debts that Iowa farmers had incurred when prices were ten times higher, and these were steadily being called in. Like most of rural America, many area banks failed and bankruptcy was as dark a plague as ever struck in the Middle Ages.

And yet, Colesburg not only survived, but apparently, learned its lesson—more than can be said for Wall Street. On September 6, 2008, when Fannie Mae and Freddie Mac were placed into conservatorship run by the Federal Housing Finance Agency, Colesburg oldest financial institution, Farmer's Saving Bank, was opening its fifth branch. Amid a national financial crisis that penetrated nearly every strata of society, in an economy where nearly ten million homeowners faced foreclosure, the Farmer's Saving Bank reports that the number of houses that they've put on the auction block is precisely zero. One reason? They maintain a consistent 80/20 rule; mortgage seekers must produce a 20% down payment before a loan is approved, and Farmer's Saving Bank will keep that mortgage in house.

Meanwhile, Colesburg farms are doing well, property values remain high, and the local banks are neither restricting lending nor recalling equity lines of credit.

And, unlike much of small town America, bemoaning the loss of mom 'n' pop shops to mega retailers like Wal-Mart and Costco, Colesburg—with a current population of around 400—has, as a community, consistently supported their own. Glance through that historical perspective again and you'll see Every's Gas Station, The Hub, Kuhlman Construction, The United Methodist Church, The Minnehaha Order Of The Eastern Star, the Constellation Masonic Lodge and St. Patrick's Catholic Church.

Now, take a walk down Main Street, 1st Street, Church Street in 2012 and you'll see these same establishments today. Some of the proprietor's names have changed (but not all); the ledgers are now electronic, not carefully compiled paper, and prices, dues and tithes are a bit higher, but otherwise, there is a sense not so much of a time warp or a time capsule, but of a time harbor—a reminder of our cultural glory days, of who we were and who, in large part, the people of Colesburg still are.

This isn't about stagnation, you see; this is about mettle. It's about perseverance, loyalty and sensible, sustainable conservatism.

It is about belonging.

*

If anyone can truly be said to 'belong' to Colesburg, Iowa, it is Fred Phelps who, along with relatives and others, was part of the committee of seven who assembled, edited and published the above-referenced 1993 'History of Colesburg'. Born in 1938, Fred's Colesburg breeding is as impeccable as any Royal pedigree and can be traced with fine-tuned accuracy back to 1823; doubtless, it preceded that, but the records are gone.

His father, Otto Ray Phelps, was born in 1906 and like his forefathers, farmed grain in the rich soils and loamy till of Eastern Iowa; to supplement the family income he drove a school bus and worked with a friend to build many of Colesburg's most enduring and solidly constructed houses. The quality of their output was in direct proportion to what Fred refers to as 'a meticulous and particular methodology'.

And why not? Throughout most of history, technological progress came from the upper strata of societies: Archimedes—inventor of the water screw, a battle-ready heat ray and ship-sinking claw—was a cousin of the king of Syracuse; Da Vinci was the son of a wealthy Florentine notary; Hero—inventor of a rocket-like reaction engine in 50 AD—was an in-demand mathematics lecturer at the famous Library at Alexandria and Benjamin Franklin was a statesman and a successful Philadelphia publisher.

But the industrial revolution changed all that, and with the advent of mechanical farming, the business of running an agricultural operation became, as the saying goes, *'10% growing things and 90% fixing things that break.'*

To survive, farmers of the nineteenth and twentieth century had to develop jack-of-all-trade skills that covered a wide array of disciplines— engineering, architecture, plumbing, animal husbandry—all bound together with practical nature and commonsense approach to the endless onset of difficulties. It was the only pathway to success.

As a result, the multitude of world-changing inventions conceived during this period came, in the main, from simple people in rural areas not only identical to Colesburg, but many within a few hundred miles of it. Henry Ford, for example, was born on a farm in Dearborn, Michigan and spent his early years in the barns and fields; Thomas Edison sold vegetables in Ohio; the Wright Brothers—neither of whom had a high school diploma—honed mechanical expertise by their years spent in a tiny Dayton, Ohio bicycle shop working printing presses, gears and motors.

Midwestern farmers in the era of Otto Phelps—as well as Fred's maternal grandfather Harbaugh—made ends meet through agrarian ingenuity, pastoral perseverance and an ocean of farmer's sweat equity.

Says Fred:

'My grandfather was a 'truck gardener'. After he retired from farming, he began to grow potatoes for the community. I can see him now, in my mind's eye, toiling in an enormous potato patch. He would also get huge shipments of muskmelons and watermelon, and before I was old enough to go to school, I'd help him load the old Model T Ford to the brim, and we'd make twice-daily trips to the countryside, where people were eager to buy the produce. We'd go west one morning and north the next, and in the afternoon, repeat the trips to other communities. We avoided the hilly country east of town, where, sadly, families were desperately poor. Folks there often lived like they had in previous centuries, in log homes without floors.

South of town was a Catholic enclave, and that was one of our favorite spots because people tended not only to be more wealthy, but had plenty of children, so they'd buy more melons!'

He paints an enviable, bucolic portrait of his early years in Colesburg, where rough spells were sutured together with frugality (his grandmother used to wash the porch with the dish water) and where prosperous times were shared with kin, neighbors and Church.

And yet, the theme adhered to which appears as frequently in Fred's reminiscing is the timed and rigid schedule adhered to by himself especially by his maternal grandparents: Lunch at eleven, supper at four sharp, and no deviation, ever. This is a town where most residents shared a Northern European/British ancestry.

Recall that the human view of time as being asymmetrical (essentially, an arrow pointing steadfastly toward the future) is a relatively recent phenomenon, and that, as a rule, farmers through history have viewed time as a cycle. One plants at a certain time in the spring, harvests at a specific time in the fall, and the following year—and the year after that, as in all the preceding years—it all happens again.

Fred was, of course, expected to follow in the silt-soiled footsteps of his father, his grandfather, his great-grandfather Alpheus (who died the same year his father was born) and carry on the tradition that had sustained Colesburg—indeed, nearly all of Iowa (which in 2011, had 30 million acres under tillage and produced 2.4 billion bushels of corn) essentially since the prairie was first settled and tilled following the Louisiana Purchase. It was, in fact, this agriculture-based society that earns Iowa her nickname: *'The Food Capital of the World'*.

When it came to Fred embracing his reserved spot amid the continuum of Phelps agronomy, there was but a single small fly in the ointment:

In his own words: "I hated farming to the 'nth' degree and wanted absolutely nothing to do with it."

So, that was that, and Fred's actual career path, however unusual for an Iowa farm boy in the fifties, was nonetheless, perhaps inevitable. Throughout his childhood, when school let out for the summer, when most of the sons of Colesburg farmers were getting initiated to 'the life', Fred was taken to Iowa City, where he'd spend vacation time at the University Hospital undergoing surgery after surgery for a congenital condition; treatable then, though not nearly as effectively as it might have been today.

He was born with a bilateral hare lip and cleft palate, and this became his earliest cross to bear; and not only for him, but remarkably—or explainably—for a number of his cousins born that same year with an identical condition. He reports no incidences of it in previous generations, although there have been several since. This leads to an obvious question: Was the cause of Fred's circumstance the luck of the draw? Was it DNA or was it the result of environmental reasons more sinister? Maternal exposure to pesticides is listed as a potential cause of *cheiloschisis* and *palatoschisis* in several studies.

Whatever the cause—genetics, ecotoxins or sheer luck-of-the-draw— Fred dealt with his situation with grace, acceptance and determination. As such, he shares a legacy with other folks through history: Tutankhamen, Abraham Lincoln's son Tad, Doc Holliday, and more recently, actor Stacey Keach and comedian Cheech Marin.

It is, after all, a treatable condition provided that reconstructive surgery is initiated early. For Fred, that began more than seventy years ago, before his first day of school.

Once he started grade school, of course, the operations were restricted to the summer months, and they continued through college: His final surgery, took place while he was attending the University of Iowa— eighty flat but scenic miles from Colesburg. It was a trip he'd taken many times with his supportive parents, and a trip they'd taken themselves countless times to visit him as he recuperated.

This last operation, the culmination of his most memorable childhood experiences, was—in his words, "A leap of faith."

He was, at the time, pursuing his genuine dream: Nursing.

*

"As I said, I never aspired to, nor intended to follow the family tradition of farming. At a very early age, I'd developed an interest in the gentle, vital and life-sustaining art of nursing; a passion I can directly attribute to the staff on the U of I pediatric ward—you can imagine how lonely a young kid, away from his family for weeks at a time could get, but the nursing staff never let me feel that way. They would allow me to do different things to 'help them out', and that gave me an incredible sense of my own value and worth at a time I might otherwise have spent feeling sorry for myself. As the years went on, I grew older than most of the other kids that were coming into the ward, and there was more and more I could do to legitimately be of service to the staff. It helped me determine pretty quickly that nursing would be my life's work.

It's a decision that I know, to this day, was both wise and honorable."

...It was decision that his parents knew instinctively was the right one, also—and encouraged him along each step of his subsequent journey. That journey which, with all its accompanying highs and lows, began in September 1956 in Dubuque, Iowa at the Finley Hospital School of Nursing as a three-year diploma nursing program. Once he'd tucked that certificate under his belt, he spent a longer stint at both the V.A. and the University Hospitals in Iowa City working toward his Bachelor of Science degree in Nursing.

Along the way, he experienced what was, up to that point, the single most significant experience of his lifetime: He met a fellow nursing student and Bachelor of Science candidate Ellen who'd come from an Illinois rural farming community similar to his own:

"A mutual friend of ours thought we should meet," he reminisces. "Our first date was in July of 1962—I took her to The Lark Supper Club in Tiffin, Iowa, then the nicest place to eat in the Iowa City area...

"We just seemed to 'hit it off'—I can't think of a better way to put it. Although, considering that I was the only male student in a class of two hundred nursing students, there may not have been a lot of options! We were both 24 at the time, an age where we were a bit older than was the local custom to get married, but we didn't waste much time..."

In fact, they were married on December 16, 1962. And today, fifty years later? Still going strong!

Following graduation, the couple moved to Quincy, Illinois, where Fred became the first male nurse ever to teach at the Blessing Hospital School of Nursing—he mentions with some amusement that he was hired on probation because the school administrators didn't think a man was capable of teaching female nursing students; their nursing program had, in the past, never even had a single male student. He points out with some satisfaction that he later became Director of Nursing Services at Blessing Hospital.

The years between 1962 and 1967 passed serenely for the Phelps's: It was the sort of idyllic, hard-working Midwestern existence that is captured in 1960's television programs. They purchased and renovated a two-story brick home on Quincy's south side—an area known colloquially as 'Calf town' because the original German settlers had once penned cattle there—and worked together to restore the hardwood floors on the main floor and to convert the summer kitchen, where women traditionally cooked in the most intense heat of summer, into a showroom for Fred's lifelong hobby: antiques.

"We called the shop—appropriately—'The Summer Kitchen Antiques'. It was a little side job for us; I had a friend who was a physical therapist at the hospital. We used to buy old furniture and restore it. We'd show the pieces in my shop and split the profits on anything that sold..."

Although children were not on the couple's agenda due to a concern that Fred's clefting deformity was genetic and might be passed along to their kids, they enjoyed all the hopes, anticipations and dreams for the future that so characterized their generation as they forged their lives along the meandering banks of the Mississippi.

There was, as it happens, only one item on the American political stage in the late 1960's—a single fly in the ointment—that might have upset those dreams.

And in the most invasive manner that one could imagine, it did.

Vietnam.

***

As required by law, Fred registered with the Iowa Draft Board in 1956 when he turned 18, but was—understandably—classified I-F: Physically Unfit. The military classification system had been revamped following the Korean War, and in peacetime, men born with certain physical handicaps were not allowed to serve, even if they had wanted to. In that year—a year before the Communist insurgent activity began—the United States Military Assistance Advisor Group assumed responsibility for training the South Vietnamese army. In 1960, the year that John F. Kennedy was elected President, the 'National Liberation Front for South Vietnam was formed; then-President Diem refers to them as 'Vietcong'.

Most historians agree that the turning point of American involvement in Vietnam took place on August 2, 1964. Following six months of covert U.S./South Vietnamese naval operations in the international waters of the Tonkin Gulf, three North Vietnamese PT boats allegedly fired torpedoes at the USS Maddox, a destroyer located some thirty miles off the coast of North Vietnam. A second, even more highly disputed attack, took place two days later. The resulting outrage among Americans led to 'The Gulf Of Tonkin Resolution', approved by Congress on August 7, 1964, which allowed President Lyndon Johnson to 'take all necessary measures to repel any armed attack against forces of the United States and to prevent further aggression.'

In short, the resolution allowed President Johnson to wage all out war against North Vietnam without securing a formal 'Declaration of War' from Congress.

By the following year, sustained bombing raids on North Vietnam *Operation Rolling Thunder* began, and in March, 1965, the 9th Marine Expeditionary Brigade arrived to defend the US airfield at Danang.

Troop strength quickly grew to around 200,000 soldiers, and the first 'conventional' clash of Americans in the Ia Drang Valley led to heavy casualties on both sides.

The stage had been set for prolonged combat in this steamy global flashpoint—a country whose cause, history and even name was largely unknown to Americans at the time.

By the end of the decade, it is safe to say that 'Vietnam' was among the most talked-about nations on earth.

Meanwhile, protected by his exempt status, Fred Phelps went about his duties as Director of Nursing Services at Blessing Hospital, by his own admission somewhat oblivious to 'the ravages of war'.

By the middle of 1966, the situation in Southeast Asia had begun to deteriorate, both in the field (as shortages in draftee quotas among South Vietnamese youths made it impossible for the ARVN to meet the proposed force level goals) and at home, as the major networks made Vietnam America's first 'televised war'.

In the final month of '65, President Johnson's advisors had convinced him the only way to win in Vietnam was to deploy a massive American ground force—advice that he chose to heed.

On January 1, 1966, U.S. forces in Vietnam totaled 184,000. Twelve months later, more than 385,000 were in country, rising to a high of 586,100 in 1968, at which point a new plan was instituted wherein South Vietnamese troops were sent to pacify the countryside while U.S. and allied forces battled the Viet Cong and North Vietnamese troops.

Clearly, to reach these numerical goals, some of the original deferments and exceptions had to be re-thought—measures referred to by the Secretary of Defense as 'necessary manpower mobilization measures'. As with most machinations of the federal government, then as now, this rationalization program took place far beyond the earshot of the average American.

When Fredrick O. Phelps received his draft notice in July, 1966 saying that he'd been reclassified as 1-A, he was as shocked as anyone.

He says, "I found out later that there was a drive to draft age-appropriate, male nurses, so I had a bulls-eye on my forehead for a while before they actually pulled the trigger. This was a time when registered male nurses represented around 1% of the profession, and there were still plenty of stereotypes alive and well about who we were."

Indeed. Even today, male nurses make up only 6% of the nursing profession, and in a 2010 article in scrubs—*The Nurses Guide To Good Living*—the 'typical' nurse of the '60s is described as 'still wearing white dresses and starched nurse caps.'

Whereas we can state with certainty that Fred Phelps never wore a starched white dress, the irony of his unexpected conscription was not lost upon him: The hare lip and cleft palate, which had rendered him unfit for duty in 1956, and which had spawned his love for and pursuit of nursing, had now been the main reason for his conscription.

Fred served with honor and commitment; his love of country and loyalty to the military were unfaltering. He shared part of the country's conviction in 1967 that suggested Vietnam was a fortress against Communism that must be held at all costs. But having taken the nursing equivalent to the Hippocratic oath—the Nightingale Pledge—he understood the value he could bring to wounded soldiers on the front lines.

What follows is the grueling, gritty, gutsy story of his experiences during the bloodiest years of Vietnam: 1967 – 1968.

Introduction: The Vietnam War, Advisors to Tet: The Johnson Era

Between 1959 and 1975, the United States was involved in a prolonged political and military conflict in Southeast Asia, which resulted in more than 58,000 Americans losing their lives.

The war was primarily fought between the nationalists of North Vietnam—intent on unifying the country under a communist government—and South Vietnam, supported by the United States and other anti-communist forces. The goal of South Vietnam was to remain independent; the goal of the United States was to prevent the spread of communism in Southeast Asia. North Vietnam viewed the conflict as a Colonial War—an extension of the fighting which had been going on for decades with the French and Japanese.

American military advisors first arrived in Vietnam in 1950 as part of a $15 million military aid package intended to assist the French in their war against the Democratic Republic of Vietnam in what was then called French Indochina. That same year, President Harry Truman began to send air and naval support to Korea.

In 1954, the decisive battle took place at Điên Biên Phú in northwestern Vietnam. After 170 days of fierce combat in which the Viet Minh, under General Vo Nguyen Giap displayed their ability to lay siege to a large garrison, the French surrendered and later signed the 1954 Geneva Accord, agreeing to withdraw its forces from all its colonies in French Indochina. As part of the agreement, a demarcation line was drawn at the 17th parallel, dividing Vietnam into a provisional North and South.

This demarcation line proved an ultimate catalyst for American military involvement in Vietnam.

Further stirring up the tempers in the North (and much of the South) was the election of Ngo Dinh Diem, a Catholic politician in a country almost entirely Buddhist. Although he was assassinated in 1963, the tension and alienation he had spread among the South Vietnamese population led to the formation of the National Liberation Front— communist sympathizers also known as the Vietcong. Although they were ultimately equipped and directed by the North Vietnamese Army, the Vietcong were a separate front operating almost entirely in the south.

Most historians point to the August 2, 1964 Gulf of Tonkin incident, when the USS Maddox was fired upon by North Vietnamese torpedo boats, as being the cause for the onset of military hostilities between the United States and North Vietnam. Five days after the unprovoked attack, Congress passed a resolution allowing President Johnson legal justification for deploying U.S. conventional forces to Vietnam and thus led to the commencement of open warfare.

Certainly, it would be a 'conflict' (as in Korea and Iraq, there was no Congressional Declaration of War) like no other in history. From the hour of the first deployment of ground troops in March, 1965, President Johnson's professed goal was not to win, but to ensure that the United States would serve as a military backbone for the South Vietnamese Army (ARVN) until they proved able to win the war for themselves.

It was a risky strategy, especially against an enemy who did not fight conventional battles, and in the long run, it failed. Rather than committing themselves to victory, many American soldiers focused simply upon a safe completion of a 13 month 'tour of duty', and toward the end of the decade, as a stalemate developed between the two sides, a limited, if extremely vocal segment of the American public began to protest against any further escalation of the war.

The so-called Tet Offensive was launched by the North Vietnamese and the Vietcong on January 30, 1968 in a show of strength that surprised— even shocked—the American and Vietnamese military. Although the U.S. and ARVN reaction was swift and decisive, and the offensive wound up as an overwhelming defeat for the communist factions, the American public saw the action as proof that the war was not only moving in the wrong direction, but was likely unwinnable. The Tet Offensive wound up being one of the major turning points of the Vietnam War, and perhaps, among the most tragic. Despite the unquestionable victory, the show of U.S. military superiority and the literal decimation of the ranks of the Vietcong, the American media tended to portray it otherwise. This, by all accounts, raised the profile of the protestors to the point where North Vietnam, prepared to capitulate in the wake of the failure of Tet and surrender, rightly believed that without the support of the American public, the U.S. would ultimately be forced to withdraw from Southeast Asia. They decided to hold on rather than surrender.

President Johnson, who had largely escalated the war by stealth, was unable to rally public commitment to the cause in Vietnam, and this led to his decision, in March of 1968, not to stand for re-election.

Born On The Fifth of July

The Florence Nightingale Pledge

I solemnly pledge myself before God and presence of this assembly;

To pass my life in purity and to practice my profession faithfully.

I will abstain from whatever is deleterious and mischievous and will not take or knowingly administer any harmful drug.

I will do all in my power to maintain and elevate the standard of my profession and will hold in confidence all personal matters committed to my keeping and family affairs coming to my knowledge in the practice of my calling.

With loyalty will I endeavor to aid the physician in his work, and devote myself to the welfare of those committed to my care.

- Mrs. Lystra E. Gretter and a Committee for the Farrand Training School for Nurses, Detroit, Michigan, 1893

1. ARRIVALS

Sunday, July 9, 1967: Arrived here at An Khe, 340 miles north of Saigon, yesterday at about 1000 hrs.—my home for the next year. Am assigned to 616th Medical Company Clearing. It is a one hundred bed hospital capable of being increased to 140 beds. I am housed in a 20' x 40' tent directly across the street from the E.R. entrance that I share with two others: Harold Chase, a nurse and Gene Snyder, a surgeon. Both appear to be fine fellows!

It seems to be a congenial group, and we have room for a couple more. There is a sort of living room with Playboy pictures on the walls, a large collection of paperback books and a beautiful new Frigidaire combo fridge and freezer filled with thick, frozen steaks: I'm asking no question as to how they got there! The tent backs into a deep ravine filled with every imaginable type of tropical vegetation and looks like a 'happy hunting ground' for snakes... The complex itself is at the foot of a forested mountain on one side, and on the other, a heliport for the 1st Cavalry Airborne Unit.

I had planned to go to church first thing this morning, but was instead taken by our head nurse Capt. Joan De Voss to Qui Nhon to be processed in; the trip took 2 ½ hours by jeep, over beautiful but treacherous terrain. I was able to get a good idea of how the local people live, but from the stories I had heard, I was in constant fear that the Vietcong would take a shot at us.

*

An Khe

Between mid-1965 and 1968, the strategic significance of An Khe to American efforts in Vietnam cannot be overstated—the presence of the American 1st Cavalry Division, which by the mid-Sixties was no longer a conventional infantry unit but an air assault division that used helicopters as troop carriers and a primary attack fleet, shows the value that the military placed on the district. The previous year had seen a number of attacks on the base and a number of training and exercise accidents in the surrounding mountains; the war was in a 'heating up' phase.

*

Monday, July 10, 1967: I had my first introduction to nursing and the peculiar problems of a field hospital today. Was assigned with Lt. Von Miller to Ward 4, a medical ward. Not many acutely ill patients here, so I was able to get a good look at the physical set-up of the activity here. Our only real patient is a young GI with a particularly desperate story: He was with a combat unit who overran a Vietcong hospital, and afterward, he and a small group of soldiers 'liberated' all the narcotics, which he has been taking ever since. Now, he's hooked.

There are a total of twelve nurses on staff, three males and nine females. All the females are single and live up the hill from the hospital complex; their quarters is a wooden-framed building surrounded by a double row of gnarled barbed wire five feet high. They are the only women among the thousands of men here!

Al Polgardy is one of the other male R.N.s, the only anesthetist in the base. My tent-mate Harold Chase is the third male nurse; he works the

17

operating room. We are all now Captains by rank—Chase was promoted today. He's from Vermont and his wife is also an A.N.C. Captain.

The wards are all contained within corrugated steel Quonsets; all are air conditioned and connected by concrete ramps surrounded by five-foot high walls of sand bags. The mess hall is also contained within a Quonset, although the chapel is made of stone and concrete. Additionally, there is an outdoor movie theater that shows films five or six nights a week.

Our staff includes three medical doctors, two surgeons, an orthopedist, a radiologist along with a handful of enlisted men.

That pretty much sums up my world.

Tuesday, July 11, 1967: An interesting day in the I.C.U. ward with enough to keep us busy. During the night, a twenty-year-old active duty soldier was admitted; he had been in a helicopter crash and fractured his hip. He'd been due to go home in one week, poor kid.

Also, the wife of a young Vietnamese interpreter was admitted with her newborn son, who had a head full of black hair the likes of which you have never seen! We have no bassinette, so we innovated by setting up a green bed sheet in a pasteboard box and attached a roller gauze ribbon to it. The Lt. broke the only baby bottle we could find, so the baby received his first feeding from a GI tablespoon.

There was also a six-year-old local boy, who by American size standards looked about two. He'd been stepped on by a cow which broke his arm, and his parents had taken him to a Chinese 'doctor' who put some concoction on the arm that was supposed to heal the fracture and instead burned all the skin off his arm, which promptly became infected.

Also, there was another boy who had been hit by a truck and broken his leg. The two share the same bed—a common occurrence. I am told that in the rural hospitals there may be three or four patients assigned to the same bed. And to think that in American hospitals we have trouble satisfying patients with double-room accommodations!

Wednesday, 12 July, 1967: Worked on the surgical floor today. We had seven Vietnamese patients, including a small boy who had severe burns over his body he received while playing with gasoline. He also has malaria.

This is a typical picture. Most of the native people have either tuberculosis or malaria or both—they receive routine chest x-rays upon admission.

The older Vietnamese play cards with the hospitalized GIs, and language seems to be no barrier. Of special delight to these natives are our apples and oranges, neither of which, for some reason, grow here. They also love our fat yellow bananas. They grow them in abundance, but eat them small and grass green, before they have had a chance to ripen.

I finished reading *'Dr. Tom Dooley: My Story'*, a book which was not only inspirational, but perfectly describes conditions here.

Thursday, 13 July, 1967: My first day being in charge of the E.R., and I can see that I really have my work cut out for me. Things are completely disorganized and filthy. I know that this is a difficult place to keep clean, but the state of the place is absolutely ridiculous. Well, it will be different in a couple of days.

There are some enlisted men working here who have already concluded that I am a slave driver of the first degree, but they are also the fellows who aren't worth their room and board. That too will be different in a couple of weeks.

I got to know the chaplain a bit better today—he is a Methodist from Ohio named Capt. (Chaplain) and has over 21 years of service time accumulated, much of it reserve time. He has six children, two of whom are adopted, and a daughter who graduated from nursing school in New

York this summer. Apparently, he knew Bishop Webb and Bishop Ensley.

This afternoon, a Montagnard woman was brought in along with her son. They had been spotted from the air by our troops and were believed to be Vietcong, especially when they ran and sought shelter in a cave. A grenade was tossed in, blowing off the young boy's foot and supposedly killing another child whose body was placed in a plastic garbage bag. We never received it.

The mother received a severe hip injury, but both she and her son will make it.

The whole thing was a terrible, terrible error, but I am reminded that within a war zone, these things happen. Doesn't make it any easier to stomach though.

Words of Inspiration:

> *'The woods are lovely, dark and deep*
>
> *But I have promises to keep,*
>
> *And miles to go before I sleep,*
>
> *And miles to go before I sleep.'*

- Robert Frost

*

Friday, 14 July, 1967: A busy day in E.R. At about 1500 hrs. we received a ten year old Vietnamese boy who had stepped on a land mine while herding cattle. As we removed the First Aid bandages we found that he had several toes missing from his right foot—a bloody, dirty, gnarled mess. Additionally, he had multiple shrapnel wounds on his legs. Interesting thing, but throughout our entire examination, he never made a sound, but when we tried to give him a pre-op injection, you should have heard the noise! Guess it proves that when it comes to the sight of needles, kids are the same around the world.

Dr. Butterfield performed cleft lip repair surgery on a five year old girl as well; it is really rewarding to see these things done so well: It makes one feel good about being here.

We also have a forty-year-old patient in I.C.U. with a bad mycordial infarction. He's doing well, proving that we can still care for patients without expensive monitors and other fancy equipment.

Finally, our Montagnard woman was supposed to be discharged today, but she refused to leave. Apparently, days in multiples of seven are considered bad luck in her culture, so we'll let her and her son stay over another day!

Sunday, 16 July, 1967: Life and its real meaning was made just a little more clear to me today. A little ten year old Montagnard girl died in I.C.U.—the cause was starvation. She looked about three years old; her upper arms measured only three inches in circumference and all the I.V.s and other treatments we tried wound up being in vain. Unbelievable to me that such things are still happening in this advanced day and age.

*

The Montagnard people were one of the most innocent and tragic consequences of the Vietnam War.

MONTAGNARDS

The multi-tribal group collectively named 'Montagnards' by the French (meaning 'mountain people') are the indigenous population of the Central Highlands of Vietnam, numbering, before the war, 3 million people. Originally, they inhabited coastal Vietnam, but were driven to the then-uninhabited mountains by a succession of invading armies.

21

At the time that American military involvement in Vietnam began, the Montagnards were almost exclusively from the Degar tribes, which has ethnic origins among the Bahnar, Jarai, Koho, Mnong and E De sub-tribe of Vietnam, each with a unique and separate language. Having originally practiced native religions, large numbers of Degar were converted to Christianity by American missionaries during the 1930's. At the onset of the war, nearly 2/3 of the Montagnard population were either Protestant or Catholic.

To some extent, the Degar Montagnard's adherence to Christianity worked against them both during the Vietnam War and after the after Saigon fell to the North Vietnamese Army in 1975. Far removed from the Vietnamese mainstream, based on physical appearance, language, ethnic origin, and most of all, religion, the tension that began in 1958 with the Montagnard's forming BAJARAKA, a movement meant to unite the various mountain tribes against the lowland Vietnamese while strengthening their social structure, grew worse with the departure of the French. Nearly all the political independence previously enjoyed by the Montagnards evaporated.

The situation nearly spiraled out of control during the Vietnam War, as it was assumed by both the NVA and the Vietcong that the Montagnards would be more inclined to help the Americans based on what was, in general, a common religion. As indeed they did; the Ho Chi Minh trail snaked through the Central Highlands, and as this was the main route for transporting supplies and troops from the North to the South, the area became of strategic importance. The U.S Special Forces began to recruit and train young Degar Montagnard men in unconventional warfare, organizing them especially in mobile strike force battalions nicknamed 'MIKE' forces. Ultimately, more than 60,000 tribal solders fought alongside the Americans and ARVN forces in the Highlands and were, in every sense of the word, true warriors.

As can be seen in the narrative, American medical personnel Like Capt.

Fred Phelps made frequent, dangerous forays into the wilds to care for the extended families of these soldiers, who were often suffering from malaria and malnutrition. Knowing that their closest kin were being cared for with the best medical attention available went far in maintaining the Montagnard's sense of gratitude and loyalty—a human side of the Vietnam War that is frequently overlooked.

Following the communist takeover of the country, many Montagnards, rightly fearing retaliation, fled the country, many with the help of their American allies. Today, outside of the Central Highlands of Vietnam, the largest community of Montagnards in the world can be found in Greensboro, Raleigh, and Charlotte, North Carolina.

*

Friday, 21 July 1967: What a very busy day we have had; I'm really beat. We got in two small Montagnard children earlier, probably brother and sister. There was a machine gunning near their village and reports are that a man was killed—was it their father? We'll probably never know. Both kids were badly hurt in the groin and thigh and looked pretty messy when we examined them. And terribly dirty. But with surgery, we thought they would do well.

The boy, who was the youngest and most precious, went to the O.R. first and shortly, tragedy struck: He went into cardiac arrest. With open chest cardiac massage, his pulse returned, but a half an hour later, he had another arrest. Our efforts from then on were in vain, and after an hour of massage, we had to give up.

Why must the young and innocent suffer so badly during this puzzling conflict? I think this is the question I ask myself more than any other, and I believe that I will continue to do so until the answer is forthcoming.

*

Sunday, July 23, 1967: My third Sunday in Vietnam. Finally, a 'sleep in' day, but the last one until goodness knows when. Began reading Thorton Wilder's 'Bridge of San Luis Rey', then went to church, where The simplicity of the chapel, with straight wooden pews, makes worshiping rather Puritanical. The hymn 'Stand Up, Stand Up For Jesus' seemed to take on a whole new significance. I never before gave a thought as to how appropriate the words are to our own situation over here.

Stand up, stand up for Jesus, each soldier to his post,
Close up the broken column, and shout through all the host:
Make good the loss so heavy, in those that still remain,
And prove to all around you that death itself is gain.

Stand up, stand up for Jesus, the strife will not be long;
This day the noise of battle, the next the victor's song.
To those who vanquish evil a crown of life shall be;
They with the King of Glory shall reign eternally.

Tuesday, July 25, 1967: This has been a bad day for me emotionally; guess I can blame it on a slight case of depression—had not expected it to hit so soon.

We were terribly busy, with five patients in from the field, one after the other. None were battle casualties: Two were punji stake wounds, two were malaria and the other was a fractured nose. Also, a Montagnard man with a suspected case of tuberculosis along with a huge, draining pus-filled abscess on his left shoulder. There was also a young Vietnamese girl who was unconscious—she had either been hit by or fell off a Lambretta motor scooter. We took her to surgery and performed a craniotomy.

I received my first copy of the Manchester Press today. How wonderful to have a paper from home!

Wednesday, July 26, 1967: I was awakened today at around 2300 hrs. by Harold, who was frantically shaking me. It was raining hard outside, and I finally gathered that he was shouting, "Attack alert! Attack alert!" What a jolt to the old constitution! I got out of bed as quickly as I could, threw my fatigues on over my pajamas, and didn't even bother to tie my boots! The hospital had been mortared just two nights before, so we were all jittery, not knowing if the alert was for real or just another training exercise.

I headed directly to my assigned post, and found that because of the alert, all light was strictly forbidden, so it was darker than pitch. Fortunately, the 'all clear' sounded after about fifteen minutes, and our relief can be imagined.

Unfortunately, I learned that during the night, the little girl who had been struck by a Lambretta died. It may have been a blessing, since she was not expected to be mentally functional again.

Thursday, 28 July, 1967: It's downright cold! Who would have believed it? The last of my thoughts would have been that we would be chilly over here.

And what a day! The second busiest in the E.R. since the hospital was founded back on May 8. It's now 2130 hrs.—just received a stab wound victim, which makes number 118 patients today, not counting the nine that were brought in shortly before midnight. All nine had gunshot wounds and all were taken directly to surgery. A terrible thing: They had been setting up camp and heard noises in the bush; they called for backup on the radio, and when the assistance came, they fired on the soldiers by mistake—something that happens all too frequently.

Also, a Vietnamese woman was admitted with gunshot wounds. She had been spotted around the perimeter at around 0200 hours and she is no doubt a Vietcong. She'll be evacuated tomorrow to Qui Nhon tomorrow where they have a prisoner ward. I listened to the interrogation, my first. She wouldn't talk, not even to give her name.

She was a real corker—her legs were scarred from previous gunshot wounds. She must have been involved with the Vietcong for a long time.

*

CIVILIAN COLLUSION WITH THE VIETCONG

Primarily a peasant militia that came and went by night, terrorizing the local population with a strategy of murder, kidnapping, torture and general intimidation, the People's Liberation Armed Forces (better known as the Viet Cong) wore civilian clothing and often faded back into the populace by day.

Such tactics had a primary advantage: American and ARVN forces, passing through villages, hamlets and rice fields, did not recognize them as combatants.

The Vietcong were notorious for conscripting labor from the local population, and villagers were forced to work in the construction of fortifications and as supply and munitions carriers; single women transported rice and men under 45 carried wounded Vietcong and NVA from the battlefields.

Not all the labor was forced however, and the VC found many willing volunteers for their cause among the South Vietnamese. This was due in part to the steady messages of anti-American propaganda that the VC spread through the hamlets under their influence, but often because they were themselves the sons of these villages, with mothers, fathers and siblings still living there. Often, the extended family would pitch in to ensure an added measure of support and safety for their soldiers.

Often, this took the form of arms production in hidden factories, many underground, where powder from dud bombs was repackaged into form of grenade, petard and mine.

Of course, this was extremely frustrating for the American military, and added to a sense of paranoia and, frequently anger experienced by GIs who knew they were charged to protected citizens that in some cases were colluding with the enemy to put them in harm's way.

*

Sunday, 30 July, 1967: I was in charge of the Intensive Care unit today, and tonight, am I bushed! It's a long day to be on the ward and not being able to leave at all.

Another tragedy: A young G.I in at about 1700 hrs.; he had been on guard out on the perimeter and was shot in the chest. He died within minutes of arrival. Turns out he was to have left for home tomorrow. I can't imagine how this unbelievable bad luck will affect his parents.

Tuesday, 1 August, 1967: An anniversary day for me: A month ago today I left the Cedar Rapids airport for Vietnam! Almost in celebration, it was a slow day with nothing of real interest taking place. We did get a few patients in from the field, but they were not too bad off. Three with malaria; one had a temperature of 105° F when we took him to E.R.

Lots of letters from home, from Ellen, the folks, Aunt Stella, etc, and a box of Fanny May candy from the Burkholz's. It feels great to be up on all the Colesburg news! I sent Ellen an airmail package that contained an Omega watch I bought her at the PX.

Thursday, 3 August, 1967: The chaplain, his assistant Martin Mullally and I went for a jeep ride around the green line (perimeter) of the compound today. What an experience! We covered some very rough and mountainous terrain; sort of spooky to say the least. With five rows of barbed wire, land mines and the huge machine guns that make all the harassment noises at night, I don't see how anyone could make it through into the camp, but I suppose anything is possible.

Friday, 4 August, 1967: We are full to overflowing, and will have to evacuate around 25 patients tomorrow—we simply need the room. We received twelve more wounded men today at around noon. Ten were GIs, but two were confessed Vietcong. One had both feet pretty much mangled from a land mine and the other had abdominal wounds and a broken hip. We will treat them just the same. Due to volume of injuries coming in, we are forced to go back to 12 hour shifts six days a week.

This afternoon, I received a package from Ellen. It contained a wonderful box of plastic medicine cups that will certainly be put to good use—the entire ward rejoiced since we had none. They are performing a cesarean section on a Vietnamese woman right now.

We also had another accidental shooting victim in, but he never made it to our unit—he died on the operating table with a bullet in his liver.

And so life, as well as death, goes on in the Republic of Vietnam.

Tuesday, 8 August, 1967: A soldier from the South Vietnamese army was admitted today. He had stepped on a Vietcong-made landmine on a path he had walked on a half hour before. It goes to prove the basic lesson of survival over here: Never travel back to a destination on the same path on which you left—you never know who is watching you from the tall grass or the ditches. The man lost one leg in surgery and the other is in poor condition.

A little R & R this afternoon, though! Some majors and lieutenants from a transportation unit furnished and prepared about 50 pounds of venison on the grill for about 35 of us. They had killed two deer last week along with a tiger. The meat was unbelievably tender—because the deer are fed on rice, or so I am told.

Wednesday, 9 August, 1967: 19 GIs in from the field around noon—most were fragment wounds. Later in the day we received word that the 15th Medical Group was being transferred to the front lines, which means that they will not be operating or dispensing sick call any longer. Consequently, we will be seeing up to 200 patients in the E.R. each morning. This will be in addition to the 125 or so immunizations we give daily. With only two surgeons and a single internist, we can count on being overwhelmed from here on out.

A young Vietnamese girl of around seven years old was brought in this evening. She had been hit by a military truck and was dead on arrival. The poor little thing never had a chance.

Thursday, 10 August, 1967: Finally, a sleep-in day! And how wonderful it was to be able to stay in bed until 0930! After getting up, I did my bi-weekly wash and got my hair cut. Slept some more this afternoon, then read the entire 12 essay series 'The Twelve Seasons' by the American naturalist Joseph Wood Krutch. Quite intriguing to read.

Received a letter from Aunt Opal, and that's about all that happened. A very quiet and relaxed day, and I needed it badly, believe me!

Saturday, 19 August, 1967: Had an unusual number of patients in E.R. today, starting with a small Vietnamese child who died from causes as yet unknown; also, a little boy with a temperature of 106° F. Surgeons discovered that he'd had a ruptured appendix for the past several days.

We delivered baby number eleven for a Mama-san through a C-section, and later, treated a GI who had both falciparum and vivax malaria. It's extremely rare to see someone with both types.

Letters arrived today from Lt. Pat Talbot of Fort Knox, an eleven-pager from Ruth Birkholz, a long one from Carolyn, one from the Earl Mosers and a precious one from my young niece Elizabeth. So, the mailman blessed me today, and I really have nothing to complain about.

I wound up playing bridge with Irvin Bruce, Martin Mullally and Harold Chase. It's very humid tonight and tough to sleep.

Monday, 21 August, 1967: I had one of the most horrifying experiences of my life tonight—one that I am sure will stick with me for a long time to come.

Shortly before dusk, I was standing in front of the Emergency Room entrance talking to our orthopedic doctor. I noticed that his eyes were getting redder and redder, and suddenly, they began to water profusely. And suddenly, my own eyes began to burn and I felt myself beginning to get dizzy as my throat began to close up. We both reached for each other, realizing that something serious was occurring, and were able to help one another across the street to my tent, where I had the foresight to keep my gas mask.

Indeed, it was a tear gas attack, and we never found out where it had come from—the enemy, or our own 'friendly fire'. I am writing this about five hours after the event. My mouth tastes bitter and at times, I am a little light-headed.

The horror of those few minutes is enough to remind us that the extra combat pay we receive over here is well deserved.

Sunday, 27 August, 1967: This morning we did chest surgery on a Korean soldier shot at the An Khe pass, a member of the Tiger Unit. Things are heating up with the national elections in South Vietnam just a week away. An attack yesterday killed two and wounded 40; all were evacuated to Qui Nhon.

We had a briefing with Major Tuttle, the Commanding Officer, who said that he would be surprised if we made it through the week without being mortared or rocketed.

This evening, we enjoyed a buffet supper at the Red Hawk officer's club. It's a beautiful building, and our officers are to be inducted as honorary members since we don't have an officer's club of our own.

Sent out 18 letters today after church!

Monday, 28 August, 1967: Another day to remember for a long, long time. This afternoon around 1700 hours we admitted a fellow GI who had been pulled into a power saw by a rope. His right hand was completely severed and the arm was severely lacerated between the elbow and the shoulder, just barely attached. He was given enormous amounts of IV fluid and blood, then taken to the Operating Room where they operated until nearly midnight. They had packed the hand in ice in the hope that it could be reattached, but the arm was much more damaged than the surgeons had anticipated and they gave up on the idea. By far the bloodiest injury I have seen so far.

Tuesday, 29 August 1967: The GI with the arm injury appears to be doing well this morning. The circulation in his lower arm appears adequate for now, but it will be a while before we see what the final result will be.

Otherwise, an uneventful day, other than the fact that I moved out of my tent. It will be dismantled to make way for a permanent building which will be a welcome change, believe me!

Friday, 1 September 1967: The first day of another month; I left home two months ago today! The time has passed rather quickly but it still would be nice to be home.

They had a piece of cake with three candles for me in the mess hall, and the rest of the day was pretty routine until 1800 when all the officers went to the 228th Aviation officers club and spent a delightful evening.

Cocktails of fresh baby shrimp and celery stuffed with creamy sharp cheese. Dinner was filet mignon, tender and juicy, fried potatoes, lettuce and tomato salad with six different kinds of dressing, hot homemade rolls. The club had white tablecloths on the tables with red candles that cast a ruby glow throughout the room. Waiters served red wine and sherry with the meal, after which there was a set of light entertainment.

Totally, the evening was a wonderful and beautiful one for my 29th birthday 12,000 miles from home.

Saturday, 2 September 1967: I had hoped to spend today recuperating from the party, but it was not to be. Hell broke loose at 1800 hours.

A convoy of GIs were traveling from An Khe to Pleiku, and about fifteen miles out, they were attacked by the Vietcong. We were told that of a 100 truck convoy, 60 trucks were damaged. In the E.R., we received forty wounded—some very seriously. It was terrible, and I hope to never see anything like it again, but I probably will.

We were dealing with fragment and shrapnel wounds to the face eyes, legs—and entire bodies. Arms nearly severed and legs with multiple fractures. During the night, another truck stopped in front of the E.R., and as we rushed to offer immediate treatment, the driver said, 'No hurry-they are all dead.'

How horrible to see these young men, fully clothes, wearing combat boots, all lying in rows on litter in the backs of the truck, lifeless. They will be going home at last, but with a military escort.

The Protestant and Catholic chaplains knelt by the side of each body, providing last rites and prayers, an image will occupy an indelible place in my memory, as will the thought of these same men passing between litters on the Emergency Room floor filled with wounded soldiers, counseling and reassuring. I recall holding the trembling hand of a young GI, who confided in me through tears, 'My driver was killed—there wasn't a thing I could do to help him.'

A lot of the injuries were to the faces of these men, and some of them will never see again. The very gravest of the wounded were evacuated to Qui Nhon for treatment. I could go on for hours telling of minor, but important interpersonal relationships I developed with the injured men in those first few critical hours, or those I observed from my vantage, but I will close by saying how impressed and moved I was by the diligence of our team, who worked all night to do what they could to make the experience, as horrible as it was, as easy as possible for these brave soldiers. In the end, of the forty men admitted, we lost thirteen.

Sunday, 3 September, 1967: Ironically, the news reports of last night's incident were as follows: 'A light attack near Qui Nhon resulted in minor injuries, moderate damage to the convoy and an unknown number of the enemy killed.' The inaccuracy of the report sickens us all.

The bulk of the day was spent doing inventory and preparing records to replace supplies after last night's deluge of injuries—it is difficult to overstate the quantity of equipment and supplies required in such cases.

I went to church this morning and nearly fell asleep—that's how exhausted I am after the last 24 hours of work.

Wednesday, 6 September, 1967: Everything was very quiet this morning with the usual number of patients seen. Then, around 2:30 in the afternoon we were alerted to some trouble that had happened in the field and we should prepare ourselves for a number of severely wounded casualties within the hour. Around 3:00, the first of them arrived, and another two shortly afterward. Blood was everywhere, and one was receiving oxygen already—this last one was a Captain in the Aviation Corps and had received massive injuries to the head and brain and regrettably, he died within fifteen minutes of admittance. Another soldier appeared ashen in color and his skin was clammy and cold; it was soon decided that his injuries—which included neurological damage—was something that we were not equipped to treat. They were evacuated by helicopter to the 67th Evacuation Hospital in Qui Nhon, about fifty miles away, and I was chosen to accompany them.

Meanwhile, the third man was taken to the operating room with a ruptured stomach and bowel. Although three surgeons scrubbed for the procedure, which also involved working on external injuries to the man's legs and head, it was ultimately decided that he would also benefit by going in the same helicopter to the larger installation.

My first medical evacuation was incredibly intense and fascinating. Between the two patients we had three separate intravenous feedings running and three different pints of blood going all at the same time. One GI was losing massive amounts of blood from his thigh wound. It took about twenty minutes to get to the Qui Nhon hospital, and in that time, we had given the soldiers about ten pints of blood, fed without I.V. standards—we had to hold the bags in the air by hand, squeezing them to force the blood in at a more rapid rate than gravity would allow. I took their pulses with the other hand.

Besides myself and the anesthesiologist, the helicopter's co-pilot was occasionally able to help; there was also a medical corpsman assisting the anesthesiologist. Two machine gunners on opposite sides of the craft were keeping a sharp eye on the countryside below. Nearly the entire time we flew at around 3200 feet at a speed of 120 knots, so not much time was wasted. Even so, by the time we arrived at the Qui Nhon helipad, my arms and legs were numb.

As we neared Qui Nhon I was able to look out over the South China Sea—a beautiful sight indeed.

Between the sea and the mountains, there was only enough room for a landing strip and the hospital, which I assume is the case for security reasons.

During the return trip—understandably more relaxed—I was able to appreciate some of the amazing Vietnamese landscape. Actually, it was a thrill to view the changing terrain that led up to our home base. It's very mountainous country, most of them steep and rugged-looking from the hair. There's a river, and leading off from it are numerous villages surrounded by rice paddies—little checkerboard areas filled with rice in various stages of development. The color in these plots ranged from lush green to drab, dry and desolate yellow brown. We could also plainly see areas where there had been severe fighting, as great patches of forest were completely burned away and barren.

I must mention that these injuries and all the subsequent activity was the result of an accident: A plane had a rough landing and the weapons it was carrying exploded. Another potentially preventable tragedy, and I am reminded of the value and shortness of life.

Sunday, 10 September, 1967: Lt. Erv Bice sang *'Be Still My Soul'* in church this morning—he truly has a remarkable voice. He has a music degree from a University in the south and aspires to become an opera star some day. I believe he will make it!

We had the most gorgeous rain this afternoon with the sun shining brightly the entire time. It was followed by the most magnificent rainbow I recall having ever seen; it was so brilliant with all of the colors distinct, forming a complete arc across the sky and touching the ground on either side. This was just another wonder to discover in Vietnam, like the incredible sunrises and sunsets. How can a country with so little offer so much in terms of beauty?

Monday, 11 September, 1967: Charlton Heston came to visit the troops today. He was supposed to have been here at 1100, but didn't show up until noon, when most of us had gone to chow. So, we missed him!

Later in the day, we had a large number of newly diagnosed venereal disease patients. The usual treatment after a positive diagnosis is established is 2.4 million units of Procaine penicillin for three days. One GI returned after an hour with one of the most violent penicillin reactions I have ever seen. Had he not returned to the E.R. when he did, I have no doubt that he would have died.

Jim Manion and I received confirmation that our leave was approved. We'll head out on 23 October, but where to, I don't know! Our choices are pretty wonderful: Singapore, Kuala Lampur, Bangkok, Tokyo... We'll find out.

*

Charlton Heston and Vietnam

During the course of Vietnam War itself, Charlton Heston—then one of the most recognized actors in Hollywood—opposed American involvement, although he was courteous and respectful to the troops. He was himself a veteran of World War II.

In 1969, the Democratic Party approached him and asked him to run for the U.S. Senate, which he very nearly did. In the end, he decided he could not give up acting.

He visited the troops in Vietnam three times; once in 1966, again in 1967 (the visit that Fred references) and in 1968.

By the early '80's, Heston had changed his political affiliation from Democrat to Republican. When asked why he had changed parties, he replied, "I didn't change. The Democratic party changed."

He campaigned for Republican Presidents Ronald Reagan, George H. W. Bush and George W. Bush, and in 2002, six years before his death, he published the following open letter to Vietnam War veterans:

March 20, 2002

Dear Vietnam Vet,

I know I've written a number of you over the years, but when asked recently by Mr. Cunningham to write, I thought I'd do just that.

Our magnificent country would not have endured had it not been for those gallant citizens who were willing to stand in harm's way on behalf of all of us. I served in World War II, my father served in World War I. Others, like you, took arms when necessary after us.

I'm deeply grateful to you, and all the others, for defending all of us and want you to know that I will never forget the family and friends who also served through you. God bless you—God bless your family. May God's grace keep you in His peace, now and forever.

Cordially,

Charlton Heston

*

Thursday, 14 September, 1967: After the magic hour of midnight, I will have exactly 290 more days left in my tour of Vietnam. A pleasant thought—the fewer the better.

Today was a day off and I slept until eight o' clock—a rare treat. My day usually begins at precisely six AM and ends around 10 or 11 PM. This morning, two jeep-loads of us went out to the west of the unit to one of the Montagnard refugee camps. It was my first trip there, and one that I have been wanting to make for a long time. A very interesting and educational experience. There were two doctors, three nurses, a medical service corps officer, three corpsmen and the chaplain. Our main mission was a MEDCAP (Medical Civic Action Program) visit. The 'village' was basically a make-shift area for about two hundred Montagnard people who have been run out of their homes by the North Vietnamese army. They are living in army surplus tents to protect them from the sun and the heat, which at this time of year can approach 130° F.

The Montagnards are among the most primitive people on earth, and in their villages, they must have had some sort of culture and way of earning a living, but now that they are displaced, and could bring nothing with them, they are living in the most abject poverty imaginable—like hogs, to be perfectly honest. Most of the children have no clothing whatsoever, and maybe they never did. The men wear beads around their necks and a loin cloth—nothing more. The women have earrings and various beads along with a cloth wrapped around the lower part of their body. Occasionally they cover the top part of their bodies, but this is rare. There are only six tents, so thirty to forty of them huddle inside each with nothing to eat but what they can scrounge up from the countryside and the rice we give them. The stench inside the tents is nearly more than one can stomach—there are sick people of all ages laying around inside the tents beside small fires over which the people do their meager cooking, using small black pots.

We brought along a crate of red apples and some C-Rations, and you should have seen the smiles on the faces of the children. Some, I am sure, had never seen an apple before.

Our main function while there was to develop some sort of treatment program for them—they have an absolutely abominable variety of diseases that most of us have only seen in medical textbooks prior to this. We hold a medical sick call and see as many of them as possible in the short time we have there. We can't do much, but anything we can do helps. At least the people are receptive and friendly, which is why they fall so easily for Communist propaganda. They consider us 'Great White Medicine Men' and anything we give them, even a couple of aspirins, is seen as a miracle cure.

Everyone, nearly without exception, has malaria, and have had it since childhood. With chronic malaria, enlarged spleens are seen, which is why the children have greatly distended abdomens.

Also, many of the people have open, draining sores and are so covered with flies that it is tough to keep from getting nauseated. One women was diagnosed with elephantiasis, a disease which causes the extremities to become oversized and hideous-looking.

Worst are the children who are literally starving to death. They have no way to fend for themselves, and the others are so hungry that they rarely share. We saw several today, too weak to sit up and so caked with filth that we took a bucket of water and a bar of soap to him and washed him by hand. Then, slowly, we fed him some C-rations which he took to like a starving bird, which is nearly what he looked like.

Nearly everyone had some form of disease caused by malnutrition and vitamin deficiency: Scurvy, beriberi, pellagra and rickets.

Some day off!

We intend to return weekly to the camp bringing crackers, C-rations, medicine, etc. And remain thankful for the things we do have, even in the midst of war.

Friday, 15 September, 1967: I received a package from Ellen this morning containing a book for my birthday, real lemon in a rubbing alcohol bottle, sweetener, Fresca and more. It all came through in great shape with none of the paper torn or anything. She mailed it on September 5th, so it takes about ten days for these things to get through.

Sunday, 17 September, 1967: To church this forenoon, and found a better crowd than normal. I was off this morning for my half-day and went to work at 1300 hrs. Almost immediately we received the body of a 22-year-old warrant officer who had been killed in action just outside the perimeter, then three more who were killed in the same exchange. They were literally full of bullet holes. Two more GIs followed along with a couple of injured Vietcong. Damn them! I am now leery of what tonight might bring. We can hear rockets being fired and many flares are appearing on the horizon, just beyond the perimeter wire.

Monday, 25 September, 1967: A slow and warm rain fell between 1500 to 2000 hours. At noon, six of us went to the Landing Zone to observe a combat air assault. Quite dramatic and interesting to see how so many helicopters, all with individual tasks, can be so well coordinated and do such an efficient job of landing, dispensing men, reloading and then taking off again. The planning must be hitch-free as all the activities must be coordinated down to seconds.

Thursday, 28 September, 1967: Today I returned to the make-shift Montagnard village for another humanitarian mission and discovered, to my great and everlasting sadness, that the young child we washed and fed had died of starvation the day following our last visit. Apparently, we had been too late to save him.

I wish that everyone back home that are so concerned with 'keeping up with the Joneses' could spend a single day among the people in this resettlement—they would have their eyes full for a very long time. For example, we brought one very sick little girl to our makeshift aid station, and found that she had worms crawling out of her rectum. And right in front of us, she vomited up a worm that was over a foot in length. And in fact, this is routine—we see these cases all the time.

Let me say some more about the Montagnard people, who, nearly to a person, are very friendly and appreciative of everything that is done for them—much more, it seems, than the average Vietnamese citizen. If we have a purpose over here in helping the people, I think it is the Montagnards.

After we finished the sick call, we traveled to a Montagnard village that had not been raided, where people had permanent structures made of bamboo and woven mats which they had occupied for quite a while. Unlike the refugees, these folks are very sturdy and robust, like I am sure our tent dwellers must have once been. They are all smiles when an American comes around and display, in every aspect of their lives, tremendous creativity and energy. Their houses are very clean and fresh-smelling; there are wild boars running loose that they must use for food. Also, water buffalo and chickens, and although I didn't see any gardens, I assume they must exist at the perimeter of the village. Through some bartering, I managed to get a beautifully polished, hand-made cross bow and a set of arrows made from split bamboo—

themselves a work of art. I also picked up an ornately carved pipe from one of the village men.

Later, we met the village elder, who shook my hand while saying, 'Me honcho', the only English he knew. We heard some beautiful music rising from a nearby hut, and requested through gestures our interest in hearing it up close. He obliged by taking us to a nearby hut and up a bamboo ladder that I was sure wouldn't be able to hold our weight, but did. Inside the hut, a group of a dozen men were playing unusual instruments made of graduated brass discs that they struck with wooden mallets. Every note on the scale was represented, tuned perfectly. When they changed songs, they replaced the discs with others tuned to the notes they wanted; the leader of the group would hum as he prepared them to choose the discs required.

This is the kind of innovation that makes the condition of those tribesmen trapped in the surplus tents, dying of starvation and preventable diseases, all the more tragic.

Saturday, 30 September, 1967: I write so much about the horrors I have encountered in this war that I worry that I have not stressed some of the beauty that can be found over here. Today was a day off, and I was invited to come along on a trip to Phan Thiet, quite a distance south of here. We traveled by Chinook—an enormously large, double rotary helicopter. An identical helicopter had been shot down the day before and our mission was to deliver new blades so that it could be repaired.

The view was simply amazing; the pilot, Major Bogart, told me that he has flown all over the world, and he truly believes that the coastal area bordering the South China Sea is the most beautiful place he has ever seen. On one side there are extremely steep, green-blanketed mountains dropping nearly directly into the ocean. Small islands are everywhere, also covered in thick green foliage. But in a small strip between the trees and the water, it looks like someone has taken a bucket of whitewash and painted a dividing line between the green and the blue: There were gorgeous sandy beaches that this place is famous for. You can clearly see the small streams that twist their way through the lowlands, supplying water for flooding the rice paddies. At the mouths of these streams, Vietnamese fishermen have place V-shaped traps; according to the Major, the fish swim into the trap and can't swim back.

Also plainly visible are those areas defoliated by some sort of chemical; necessary because the Vietcong take refuge in the thickest parts of the jungle and can be rooted out with defoliant.

*

Agent Orange

Agent Orange was the primary acetic acid herbicide and defoliant used in Vietnam to destroy the natural cover used by the Vietcong, as well as food crops, with the intent of forcing the rural population into cities. Highly effective, Agent Orange was used between 1961 and 1971 as part of Operation Ranch Hand, and derives its nickname from the color of the orange-striped barrels in which it was shipped. Mixed with jet fuel, it is estimated that over 20 million gallons was dumped on Vietnam, eastern Laos and parts of Cambodia. By the time its use ceased, about 12% of South Vietnam had been drenched with the chemical at a concentration thirteen times higher the recommended rate for domestic areas.

In 1965, it was discovered that Agent Orange was highly toxic to humans as well as foliage—a fact downplayed by the manufacturing companies. The Red Cross of Vietnam estimates that up to 1 million people are disabled or have health problems due to Agent Orange, along with 500,000 children born with birth defects.

And hundreds of thousands of U.S. Vietnam vets, who have suffered through the sad legacy for nearly forty years.

In 1965, Dow Chemical Company released a memo calling Agent Orange '...one of the most toxic materials known, causing not only skin lesions, but also liver damage.'

The memo, which did not surface until a 1990 report was submitted to the Secretary of the U.S. Department of Veterans Affairs, greatly underrated the true danger of Agent Orange to human beings, with thousands of cases of cancer, diabetes, Parkinson's disease now understood to have been caused by exposure to the toxin.

*

Sunday, 1 October, 1967: I am now ¼ through with my tour! We received word today that we would soon be visited by Colonel Boyson, the C.O. of the 44th Medical Group along with General Collins. No idea why they will be coming, but one section of the 1st Cavalry has left the compound, transferred to a more forward area to support the Marines. It is possible that they will be moving us as well.

Monday, 2 October, 1967: Since I have not yet washed into the South China sea, I figured I better write this entry quickly. We are in the middle of what I am told is a typical monsoon season in the Central Highlands of this strange, war-torn country. I am a sound sleeper for the most part, but I was awakened at one o'clock in the morning by the incredible storm, but only the rain: Strangely, there is rarely any lightning or thunder associated with the downpours. I understand that this will be the state of things around here for the next three months.

We had received word on Saturday evening that the commanding general of all medical facilities in Vietnam, along with the C.O. of our particular group, would be arriving early this morning. Our C.O. showed up last night, earlier than expected, and on schedule, the Commanding General, who is directly under General Westmoreland. Along with him were the Chief Nurse of all army nurses in Vietnam, the Chief of Medicine over the in-country army services and all of their aides and assistants. What a free-for-all! They toured the facility and the grounds, then went into a meeting so closed that even our unit C.O. was not allowed to attend. We were all confident that we would be evacuated in a soon-to-be-disclosed number of hours, likely closer to the DMZ. But, by the grace of God, we were soon told that not only would we not be moved, we would receive some additional medical support from extra doctors and nurses. The impression given was that we will soon be even busier than normal, but at least we will be staying put.

Thursday, 5 October, 1967: Our new nurse arrived today. His name is Lt. John Mosley, a graduate of Alexian Hospital School of Nursing in Chicago; he is originally from Washington DC. He'd been at Letterman Army Medical Center in California with Harold Chase, and will be a fine, sharp addition to the staff.

A young, comatose fellow was admitted this evening, and when he was being undressed, a packet of marijuana was discovered in his clothing.

Later, I began an exercise regimen that includes sit-ups, push-ups and deep knee bends. I'm determined to take some extra inches off my waist and hips.

I Dream, I Think, I Pray

I dream of days gone by,

With blue clouds in the sky.

I dream of loved ones there

At home, and know they care.

I dream of times when we were gay

And know that God had led the way.

I think of fields so lush and green,

More beautiful than most have ever seen.

I think of bright trees in the fall,

And how they heed to nature's call.

I think of men fighting here so strong and brave,

And ask that God will keep them from their grave.

I pray that I shall long be spared,

To relive once again the joys we have shared.

I pray that all these precious gifts of ours,

Will be forever nourished by heaven-sent showers.

I pray to God each day I live,

'What more have I that I may give?'

- Capt. Fred Phelps, ANC; 616 Medical Co. Clearing

Saturday, 7 October, 1967: It is just past 2230 hrs., and I am returning from making my rounds of the wards. Things have quieted down since 1900 hrs. when we had a large field evac in, most with fragment wounds. Two were Vietnamese workers who had been mistaken for Vietcong.

At noon we did a C-section on a Vietnamese woman, but unfortunately, the baby wouldn't breathe on its own for an hour and a half, so I am not sure of the outcome. We have 20 Vietnamese patients on the ward right now, five more than we are authorized to treat.

Sunday, 8 October, 1967: We were awakened abruptly at 0100; we knew it would not be a drill because we'd just had one eight hours earlier. The sky outside was ablaze with flairs and the sound of gunfire was deafening. We dressed quickly and tried to determine if the mortars were falling anywhere near the hospital complex, and finally decided to make a dash for the E.R. where I was pleased and proud to see the immediate activities that were being carried out. Within a very short span of time, all the patients were placed on the floor beneath their beds with everything—I.V.s, nasogastric suctions, etc., continuing to operate. Available enlisted men not needed in the nursing unit were detailed to Supply to issue weapons. A firmer security around the hospital was soon established.

Word came in that five people were killed in the attack and that the area where it took place has been leveled. This is where our warehouses are (were) located, so naturally, all our supplies, power and construction materials were destroyed. It will be quite a task to repair all the damage done.

We later learned that the attack had been carried out by a suicide squad; two groups of about six or seven Vietcong who cut the fence and came in from two separate locations. Numerous satchel charges had been placed at various spots, each containing about a half pound of dynamite.

'All Clear' sounded around 3:00 AM, but it was difficult to sleep; I am again reminded of the gift of life and how quickly it can be extinguished. I finally drifted off while listening to a gospel program by the Blackwood Brothers Quartet

Monday, 9 October, 1967: At about 2030 hrs. one of the corpsmen on duty came and woke me to tell that a Captain Reyda was on the phone. What a wonderful surprise! Stephen Reyda, who is at the 85th Evac Hospital in Qui Nhon, was a head nurse at Brooke Army Medical Center in San Antonio, Texas with me before either of us came to Vietnam. He arrived in country a week before me, and we have been trying to get in touch ever since. We spoke for about twenty minutes, and would really like to get together in person, but our movement around the country is understandably restricted.

Around 0030 hours, the same corpsman awakened me again along with Al Polgardy and Harold Chase saying that there had been a shooting and the victim needed immediate surgery. Lou and I rose immediately; I guess neither one of us had been too sound asleep.

It turns out that one of our enlisted men had stolen an M-14 from the orderly room and held off the other soldiers who came to retrieve it for quite a while before fleeing into the barracks. Apparently, he harassed a number of other enlisted men along the way, and finally shot one of them in the leg. The bullet missed a major artery by only a fraction of an inch. By the forenoon, he was doing well and had a sustained good pulse.

Also, a Vietnamese woman on Ward #1 had a precipitate delivery in bed this afternoon. A bloody mess; the baby died at 1630 hours. Another Vietnamese newborn died last night as well. The rate of newborn death in this country is high to begin with, but our mortality statistics in the hospital are poor.

I can't imagine what tomorrow will bring. I must say, life here is endless suspense.

Thursday, 12 October 1967: The Fifteenth Medical Group moved out today and we ended up with all their patients. Also, we received a large evac from the field and had to open up Ward #5—our last ward with additional beds. So now we are out of beds. I am just hoping that there are no more mass casualties.

In the afternoon, we did a routine visit to the Montagnard village and returned with a small orphan girl. She was in pathetic condition, the worst that I have seen, and the villagers were simply not taking care of her. Horrible—severe malnutrition, greenish diarrhea and a prolapsed rectum. It really made my heart ache. I would love to be able to take her home with me. She has big brown eyes and hair that would be lovely if taken care of—she has all the makings of a beautiful child. I have written in detail to Ellen about this in a long letter that I will further reference later in this journal.

Friday, 13 October, 1967: Friday the 13th—a good thing I'm not superstitious or I would have thought it came a day earlier for me. Yesterday was horrendous from beginning to end. Quieter so far today, although we did see 115 patients at sick call.

I went to the Judge Advocate's office this morning for information about the adoption policies of Vietnamese children.

We call her 'Orphan Annie' since we don't know her correct name. She is doing better today, although she is very, very weak. She has a hacking cough and her abdomen is quite distended. Dr. Manion put her on a liquid diet and will take a chest X-ray and perform a skin test on her tomorrow. She also seems to be itching quite a bit and is fussy this evening.

We also received a Vietcong patient who had apparently been wounded quite a while ago without treatment—he had thousands of maggots in his wounds. We took him to surgery immediately, and they had a job indeed.

Also, we got in a GI who had his scrotum shot off; his bowels were protruding. Along with two others, he had been ambushed on the An Khe pass. The other two were killed.

Sunday, 15 October, 1967: Little Annie is not well today; she is listless and sad-looking and suffers terribly from diarrhea. Despite our feverish treatment and concern, she seems to be getting worse. She weighs 19 pounds.

Her stool specimen shows copious amounts of ascaris (intestinal roundworm), amoeba and hookworm eggs. There are also a lot of fat globules, showing that her body is not absorbing fats as it should. We started her on strained baby foods in the hope that she can retain that.

She always seems so hungry, but apparently eating is not doing her any good.

Tuesday, 17 October, 1967: Returned to the Montagnard resettlement area with my good friend Dr. John Deen where we held the usual sick call. It is amazing how the number of patients has dwindled since we first went out there six weeks ago. People have made progress in building huts for themselves, and in general, are much healthier. When we first arrived, it was nothing to find two or three people dead; now, there has not been a death in three weeks. It is something that makes one feel good about what we are trying to accomplish over here.

There are, of course, still patients with weeping sores and open wounds, but they are healing rapidly. It's amazing what a little hydrogen peroxide, Bacitracin ointment and clean dressings can do. Still, it is a wonder that anything heals in this filthy environment. I assume that those who remain alive must have very strong constitutions.

Later this afternoon, I made it to the barbershop, although I hate going here as much as I did back in the states. There's always a line, and it strikes me as such a waste of time that could otherwise be spent more productively.

I managed to get my khaki uniforms arranged and my shoes polished so that they will be ready to go when we go on leave this Sunday. It seems that they do not remain polished very long! Another male nurse leaves in a few days for R & R to meet his wife in Hawaii; he informed us that he has 33,000 seconds left with the unit!!

Wednesday, 18 October, 1967: Annie remains about the same. She passed a huge male roundworm, and their eggs remain in her stool samples, which means that she must still have a female inside her.

Thursday, 19 October, 1967: This evening we took the patients to the Division Bowl to see Martha Raye from the 'Hello, Dolly' show. She was out of this world! After the show, she offered a heartwarming talk to us all; she said that the draft-card-burners back home were not even man enough to polish our boots. She received a standing ovation from nearly five thousand men!

Friday, 20 October, 1967: Had two NCO's in today hit by a white phosphorous grenade—they had burns over their entire bodies. One of the fellows had eye involvement which makes it very bad. It took us almost three hours to care for them.

Saturday, 21 October, 1967: Whew! I caught a very bad cold and it has really gotten to me. I would give anything to get rid of it before we leave tomorrow.

A day off, and I was not intending to do much but get my things together for leave. Letter from Ellen most welcome, which I was reading in my room. Then, at 1930 hrs. I heard a loud explosion nearby, and went to my door, then proceeded around the building in search of signs of fire. Nothing seemed out of place, so I went back to room where Jim Manion told me that we should go immediately to the E.R. because there had been trouble at 15th Med. I threw on some fatigues and went to emergency where we received thirty patients—20 on litters. Nearly all had fragment wounds due to a blast from a homemade grenade that had been thrown into the E.M Club at the 15th Medical Unit where they were simply enjoying a floor show by some Korean entertainers. Four of them were injured also. As usual, no one knew where the grenade had come from.

A sad way to end my last night before leave.

Sunday, 22 October, 1967: I went to the hospital early to take the morning census, then Jim Manion and I went to the airport in an attempt to get an earlier flight out of Cam Rhan Bay. Unfortunately, we didn't make it, so wound up at the airport until 1700 hrs., where at least I got a lot of reading done on the novel Andersonville, although I wound up with a sore buttocks from sitting so long on the wooden benches!

Joyously, just as I was boarding the plane, Kendall Haines was getting off. What a wonderful feeling seeing him; I am sure it is going to be a great reunion for the both of us. I am so happy that we will be spending the next few months together—it will be good for both of us. The first thing I said to him was "My, you must have been eating well the past few months"—I was surprised at how much weight he had gained! Those last few home-cooked meals seemed to affect a lot of arriving vets like that. I was sorry that I could not be there to help him settle in, but I am sure he will be well taken care of.

We arrived at quiet and peaceful Can Rhan Bay at 1900 hrs. and found it beautifully refreshing; we were then taken to the 22nd Replacement Battalion where we will be billeted tonight. The ride was also refreshing and smooth—the vehicles here don't appear to have square wheels. The 22nd is the main processing point for Americans going on leave, R & R or returning to the hallowed United States, and it is a far cry from reception center at the 90th Replacement in Long Bien! It is so clean, with mountains in the background and a large blue river separating the mountains from our area. Everything is covered with the soft, pure white sand the area is famous for. Under the full moon, I think only a Midwesterner would think that the landscape had been covered with a blanket of snow.

After having been in the primitive Central Highlands, it seems like a little slice of heaven.

I had a deep, restful sleep—I think it is the first time in a while I slept without rockets and machine guns being fired nearby.

Monday, 23 October, 1967: We arose at 0530 hrs., went to the processing center around 6:30 AM to await for the 7:30 AM flight to get our standard reservation flight to Hong Kong, where we arrived at about 1700 hrs. The terminal was large and impressive; there were Oriental Military police to guide us through. Beautiful, clean buses were waiting to take us to the briefing center as soon as we picked up our luggage.

The briefing lasted an hour, and afterward, we were taken to 'The President', our hotel in downtown Kowloon. We have a lovely, carpeted room with flush toilets!

We changed into civilian clothes since we are not permitted to wear uniforms in the street, then went to the hotel's Three Kingdoms restaurant for a wonderful meal amid a relaxed, refined atmosphere: There were china plates, tea spoons and linen tablecloths. I had turtle soup, a corned beef sandwich and for dessert—hold on to your hats—flaming baked Alaska. The entire bill came to $21.40 Hong Kong dollars, so at an exchange rate of $5.74 HK to $1.00 US, the meal was a bargain.

After eating, we toured the hotel, which covers an entire city block, doing window shopping (I priced sapphires, opals, jade and carved ivory—I'll decide what to buy later), returning to our room at 2330, where I took a wonderful, long hot water shower with the water running continually, not just when you pull the chain like it does at our base in Vietnam!

Slept well—I noticed that despite the volume of traffic, it was very quiet, and later learned that it is illegal in Hong Kong to use your car horn after dusk. It was unbelievably relaxing to sleep on a soft bed in an air-conditioned room without rockets being fired nearby. Plus, the windows are thick, and it is so quiet in the room that it is almost like I am living in the world of the deaf.

Tuesday, 24 October, 1967: This promises to be a big day full of new experiences. We spend most of it at the China Fleet Club, a large P-X-type store operated by contracted merchants, ensuring that the merchandise is of high quality. Open only to military personnel, everything is available at a discounted rate, so we wound up too intrigued to leave! Basically anything you might want can be found here, from Mikimoto pearl necklaces for several thousand dollars to Hi-Fi equipment, clothes and silver. To get here, you have to take a ferry from the mainland, which is where we are staying.

I bought an antique water cooler and some watercolor and lithograph prints from Lane Crawford (the Marshall Fields of Southeast Asia) along with some star sapphire cuff links and a ring. The folks who sold me the jewelry introduced me to the people who manage the business, and they allowed me to choose my own stones for the links and the ring. They also showed me thousands of dollars worth of other unmounted stones: A once in a lifetime experience!

We had dinner at the Siamese Starlight Rooftop Garden at our hotel, seated before a massive plate glass window through which we could see the lights of the city of Kowloom as well as the harbor, the bay and the island of Hong Kong itself—an absolutely breathtaking panorama. As we ate, a violinist and a pianist played soft dinner music; the main course was Roast Peking Duckling with orange sauce, and it was delicious, to say the least.

Wednesday, 25 October, 1967: Today I did some more serious shopping, buying linens, silks and cashmere. One of the most beautiful items was a banquet-table sized Army/Navy tablecloth made of alternating lace and embroidered linen. A dozen lace-edged napkins were included. This is the sort of cloth used in the most formal dinners of the highest ranking military officials. I look forward anxiously to the day when Ellen and I can entertain in our home and use these incredible items.

Thursday, 26 October, 1967: My, how these days go by so rapidly, and this has been another delightful one. The weather is balmy, without so much as a single disagreeable cloud in the sky since we arrived. In the morning, we returned to the island and the China Fleet Club where I mailed a pair of ginger jar lamps to Ellen. We took a guided tour of the island, and found it fascinating, beautiful and unbelievably crowded. Among our fellow passengers were a trio of nurses from Con Chi at the 12th Evac Hospital.

The tour included Tiger Balm Gardens—the Disneyland of Southeast Asia (although there is no animation)—the beautiful beaches, fishing villages where people live on small boats, and took a cable car to the highest point on the island. We were there when it grew dark, and could see the entire city of Hong Kong and Kowloom and far up the coast of Victoria Harbor, where thousands of small sailing vessels were plying their trade.

The entire fascinating day set me back only $20 HK, about $4.00 US!

Had dinner at the third floor hotel restaurant, The Hall of Nine Dragons, and was in bed by 9:30 PM. I guess us 'old soldiers' just can't take too much nightlife.

Friday, 27 October, 1967: Our last full day in Hong Kong—a city of contrasts. A few notes of interest: The government owns all the land, and building owners pay tax for the right to have businesses there. In fact, the only people who can legitimately own land are the dead: It costs around $1000 to be buried in a private cemetery, but if you are buried in a public cemetery, your remains are dug up after seven years. Also, steering wheels are on the opposite side of the vehicle than in the United States, and cars drive on the 'wrong' side of the street. Makes me nervous, but we are not allowed to drive while in country. Also, in Vietnam, officers are not allowed to drive, so I suppose I will have to take driving lessons when I return to the good old U.S.A.

We took lunch at The King's Lodge, a German restaurant in a cellar of the Palace Hotel: Boiled sausage and sauerkraut with fresh rye bread. I enjoyed it more than anything else I've tried here so far, so I guess it must be the German in me coming out!

Afterward we walked to the offices of Manchu Gems to pick up the jewelry I had ordered earlier, including my ring, cuff links and tie tack, and Ellen's gorgeous star ruby earrings and pendant, which are supercalifragilistic!

We relaxed in the hotel room for a while, then joined a 'dinner tour' of

Hong Kong as our farewell to this fine city. We dined aboard a small, yacht-like vessel, seated at a round table for six. It turned out that one of the six was a Brigadier General in the Royal Canadian Medical Corps. You could have knocked us over—it just goes to show that Generals are human too!

We leave tomorrow at 0800 hrs. By the way, my bill for the entire five night stay, including room service, laundry and the duckling and lobster dinners was $44.00 US.

Saturday, 28 October, 1967: Upon my return, I found 40 letters and 4 tapes waiting for me!

Sunday, 29 October, 1967: A lost day; I was so sick I could barely move and Jim Manion started an IV around 1000 hrs; 2000 cc of fluids.

Monday, 30 October, 1967: Worked all day, although I promise you, I didn't much feel like it.

We are on constant alert, having heard that a Special Forces camp nearby was overrun by the Vietcong and a son of a local chief killed. It may be in protest to President Ky being sworn into office, and further trouble is expected all over the country. There was some shooting on the edge of the camp—same place that was attacked two weeks ago, near where P.A. & E is located. Things are very uncertain.

But, the good news is that 'Annie' is alive and well, eating, and although she only weighs nineteen pounds, she seems much more cheerful.

Tuesday, 31 October, 1967: Happy Halloween! And, it was one year ago today that I was inducted into the United States Army at Ft. Sam Houston, Texas. What a varied array of experiences and observations have happened to me since then, some pleasant, some not. Some rewarding, others not. Still, all of them have their place and have served to make me increasingly more thankful for the things I have.

Wednesday, 1 November, 1967: As of today I have completed 1/3 of my time here in Vietnam. In two months, I will have half my time in.

Another beautiful, warm, sunny day. I don't know what happened to the monsoon rains, they seem to have simply stopped.

I was able to spend some time with little Annie this evening; when I extended my hands to her, she came right to me. She's gained five pounds and her appetite has much improved, so there is some reason to be optimistic. Finally.

Saturday, 4 November, 1967: So much for the lovely weather: It rained very hard all night and is still coming down this morning. As soon as I got to the E.R., I learned that our new chief nurse is a Major and should be arriving in two weeks. I am relieved that I will no longer have that responsibility, since I foresee a series of nasty problems in the not-too-distant future and am glad that I will not be involved in them.

The other bit of good news is that Annie now weighs 21 pounds, is smiling a lot more, and earlier today stood on her own for the first time since being hospitalized!

Sunday, 5 November, 1967: A day off. I went to church at 10:00 AM. There was good attendance today, the best of any Sunday since I have been here. Chaplain Belton delivered his first sermon today, and what a fine speaker he is. We had a simple but impressive Communion service.

On Tuesday, we will begin a daily devotional service of ten to fifteen minutes in duration, and on Wednesday we will have our first choir practice in preparation for the Tri-Faith Thanksgiving services. It promises to be a most interesting religious experience.

This afternoon, Capt. DeVos, Lt. Haines, Lt. Mosley and myself went to Lazy Acres and played some croquet. Great fun—it had been a while since most of us had played. Later, I played a round of miniature golf on the newly-constructed course that was just dedicated yesterday.

Monday, 6 November, 1967: One of the most mentally trying and physically demanding days I have spent here so far, with over 175 patients seen at sick call alone, with other business happening in the E.R. LTC Rose Straley, the Assistant Chief Nurse of Vietnam, spoke with each one of the nurses individually—among the things I requested was an assignment for further duty in the United States once I return. I also asked for the Regular Army Commission papers. My stateside preferences included teaching at MTC or MFSS at Sam Houston, Clinical Specialist Instruction at Fitzsimmons in Denver or In-Service Education responsibilities at Ft. Carson or Ft. Knox.

A few weeks ago, I mentioned an enlisted man who shot another enlisted man; today, he attempted to commit suicide by cutting his left wrist with a surgical knife. I feel so sorry for this man—he is clearly very ill and it seems that nobody has taken the time to realize this until now.

What a day. I won't need anyone to rock me to sleep tonight, I can assure you.

Tuesday, 7 November, 1967: Linen day, and gratefully, there is a bright sun without much humidity, and all my washing dried quickly—I even hung my poncho out for the first time in a while. At least I will have clean sheets to crawl between tonight.

We admitted a young Vietnamese woman this afternoon who appeared to be in a semi-comatose state. Her husband reported that she had a child about four months ago and at the time had lost a lot of blood. Apparently, she had not been well since then. Well, unfortunately the medical staff determined that it was a case of the rabies—in which case, her condition is fatal, and likely soon. There has never been a single case in all medical history of someone surviving with rabies.

Wednesday, 8 November, 1967: It was a quiet morning, but in the afternoon, things really took a turn for the worse. We received a call that we were going to receive two patients by med-evac, and soon, the helicopter was landing on the pad below the emergency room. I have

seen a lot of horrible things here so far, but nothing that could compare to this—and nearly everyone on our medical staff said the same thing.

There were two Vietnamese children, about ten or twelve, who had been hit by a grenade. One girl had her right arm completely severed and her right foot was dismembered, the leg being held in place only by a small amount of tissue at the knee. Her left leg was bent completely backward with her foot lying near her waistline. She was, of course, covered in blood and virtually unrecognizable as a human being. She took about a dozen breaths after she arrived, then died.

Her sister was in a slightly better condition and was taken to surgery immediately and is now in Intensive Care.

The woman with rabies died this evening. We knew her time was short.

It was something to consider at tonight's vesper service, our second.

Sunday, 12 November, 1967: Good turnout at church this morning, and afterward, as we returned to E.R. we learned that there had been a big military push near Pleiku, and that my roommate Lou Vinning and several of the operating room personnel had been evacuated to the front to care for patients. This is about fifty miles from here, near the place where I mentioned the truck ambush that resulted in so many casualties. Apparently, old 'Charlie' is still alive and well, and nobody knows where he will next rear up his head.

Just after noon we received a call saying that we would be receiving some 'overflow' from the battlefield—patients who could not be cared for at the 71st Evac Hospital at Pleiku, the 67th Evac or the 85th at Qui Nhon. Soon afterward we received 22 patients, nearly all requiring immediate surgery, so our two operating rooms were occupied from 1:00 PM to 9:00 PM. We stayed busy constantly, admitting, transporting to and from X-Ray, taking vital signs, prepping patients for surgery. One, a Vietnamese woman suspected of being Vietcong had a severe head injury with brain tissue coming out of her forehead. Another Vietnamese soldier was dead on arrival with a bullet wound to the chest.

The Chaplain's sermon this morning was taken from the 6th Commandment, 'Thou shalt not kill'.

I found it quite ironic.

Tuesday, 14 November, 1967: My headaches continue to get worse despite the Darvons and around midnight, I got up and went to the E.R. Dr. Lohmer saw me and did a complete neurological scan and gave me a half grain of Codeine by injection. Even so, I didn't rest well.

At least the mail cheered me up: I received a small, battery-powered Christmas tree from Ellen, and it lights up the entire room.

Saturday, 18 November, 1967: A c-o-o-l morning, and I hated to crawl out of bed to face it: The air feels like is blowing down from a huge snow bank. The initial shock of getting up is quite traumatic.

Nothing much happened in E.R. today, except that we learned some interesting facts about our patient who had slashed his wrist—the same one who had shot a fellow GI. Apparently, he enlisted with a stolen draft card and has been going under an assumed name ever since. Also, he is wanted in Connecticut for a prison escape, where he was serving a life sentence!

We continued with the hospital clean-up campaign, with a lot of painting, scrubbing and washing going on throughout the wards, the officer's lounge and the barbecue area.

Monday, 20 November, 1967: We learned today that there is still heavy fighting occurring at Dak To along the Cambodian border—a long, hard-fought battle.

We ran about 130 patients through sick call this morning, with 24 of them as new venereal disease patients. Incidents of V.D. are incredibly high; higher than I think statistics show, and those are high enough.

Annie has taken a turn for the worse, I am sorry to say. Her liver and spleen have suddenly become enlarged and there was some cardiac involvement that required digitalization. Jim believes that she may have portal ascaris—worms in the portal vein of the heart. She's having trouble breathing when she lies down. We also think that there may have been some brain damage, so the outlook is rather dim. Word is that she may be transferred to another hospital soon, so her prospects remain to be seen.

Whatever happens is God's will, I am certain.

Thursday, November 23, 1967: Thanksgiving Day, and I am reminded of one year ago when I was training at Ft. Sam Houston. I spoke to my parents at noon, then a group of us had dinner together at Wyatt's Cafeteria in San Antonio.

This year, I arose at 6:00 AM and washed the curtains from the Chief Nurse's office!

The division played two songs in front of the chapel; *'Come Ye Thankful People, Come'* and *'America'*. Even though I am away from my friends and family, I still have plenty of things to be thankful for—especially, that I am still safe after five months in country. My health remains good, and everyone back home seems to be doing fine. I have made many new friends and acquaintances here, and I am grateful that this conflict is not being waged on American soil.

Saturday, November 25, 1967: The new P-X opened today, and most of the camp went to the opening. I decided to wait and avoid the lines of people and the mobs. I washed my uniform instead!

Some really big news arrived with the mail: The Department of the Army has informed me that I have been selected for the Army Career Course at Ft. Sam Houston, set to begin in September. That means that

Ellen and I will be returning to San Antonio.

I did make a trip to the new P-X later in the afternoon, and what a place! It makes any P-X I have seen in the United States look pretty sick. It is gigantic—the second largest in Vietnam—and has anything I imagine anyone could want.

Afterward, a group of us went to the Can-Do Club for the usual Saturday night of steaks and entertainment.

Friday, 1 December, 1967: Today marks another milestone—I have completed five months in Vietnam and have seven more to go. Another month and I will have half of my 'sentence' served.

There has been a lot of activity around the perimeter lately; more than usual. I hope that doesn't mean that we are in for something tonight. The people who were supposed to go on MEDCAP tomorrow were told that it would not happen due to 'too much happening in the surrounding area'. I'm not really sure what that means except that it does not sound like a good sign.

Saturday, 2 December, 1967: Unfortunately, my prediction came true. We had just gotten started at sick call this morning when we received word that we would be getting battle casualties. And we certainly did.

Of the first group of 18, only three were our soldiers—the rest were N.V.A. (north Vietnamese Army). Most of the enemy were wounded so severely that we couldn't care for them and had to evacuate them to Qui Nhon, but we were left with enough to do that we were very busy all day long. By 1800 hrs. we had admitted thirty patients to the hospital besides those we saw in E.R. as outpatients.

I had some distressing news from Ellen regarding Jerry Baumgartner, my roommate in nursing school, and his condition; I am so shocked that I barely know what to say. It seems apparent from his symptoms that he has Hodgkin's Disease, and according to Ellen, his condition is very grave. I hadn't heard from him in a long time, and now I know why, although I don't know just what to do. If I write to him, what will I say? Why do these things happen to such a young man with a family and an entire life in front of him? I'm thinking about the countless experiences we had together at nursing school and our early careers at the V.A. Hospital in Iowa City. I remember the trip we made to Denver over Memorial Day weekend to visit Charlie Boyle; I remember how close we became when we both lived in the same trailer park during college; I remember the numerous visits to each other's homes. But most of all, perhaps, I recall our last time together, when I was home on leave before being sent overseas. What I wouldn't give to see him one last time, but it seems that this is not to be. It is God's will. At least I will have these memories preserved forever.

Monday, 4 December, 1967: Last night at around 10:30, I was awakened by Harold Chase and Al Podgorny telling me the tragic news of the deaths of four nurses in a plane crash near Qui Nhon; they had been in Pleiku to assist with the extra work load there caused by increased fighting near the Cambodian border. One of them, Lt. Kenneth Shoemaker, was a friend of mine—we did basic training at Ft. Sam Houston together, ate together several times at the Barn Door, a good restaurant in San Antonio, I recall having gone to San Marcos with Ken one Saturday. He, Danny Likens and I had spent quite a lot of time together. He had been assigned to the 67th Evac Hospital at Qui Nhon as a nurse anesthetist. His wife is expecting their first child.

The other male nurse was Lt. Jerry E. Olmstead, also a nurse anesthetist. He was with the 85th Evac Hospital and was from Clintonville, WI, near Green Bay. I believe he was married just before leaving for the Army. The other nurse killed was a Lt. Lane.

There were also two operating room nurses killed. These are the first nurses killed in Vietnam.

Major Ebert has reported that the plane crashed into the side of a mountain and all 22 on board were killed. Apparently, the crash had occurred last Thursday at 2:15 PM—the time was identified by the calendar watches of the victims which had stopped at that time. It was only yesterday that they could retrieve the bodies due to hostile fire received by rescue workers. It is reported that the bodies were spread over a wide area, with some found in trees.

The tragedy continued later today when we received a Montagnard girl of about 15 who had been shot in the back of the head. Some of the staff here remember her as one of the most friendly natives at the village. It is believed that she was hit by enemy fire. She was alive, but convulsing when she came in, but on her own strength, she was able to live for quite a while after being taken to E.R., but unfortunately, there was nothing we could do for her.

Wednesday, 6 December, 1967: At about 1000 hrs. today we received four wounded Vietnamese by Med-Evac chopper—three children and an older man—all with grenade fragment wounds. We treated them despite not knowing who they were, where they came from, or how they had been injured.

Thursday, 7 December, 1967: We had choir practice this evening, and the turn-out was not so good. And yet, how well the voices of those present blended! Especially in 'Silent Night, Holy Night'. It sounded so nice that our director, Erv Brice, requested that we re-sing it at the close of practice, saying, "If Norman Luboff could hear us now!"

Later, we had our first nurses staff meeting conducted by Major Ebert, and everyone was pleased with the way it turned out. Among other things, a committee was chosen to plan our Christmas party.

Saturday, 9 December, 1967: A big day at the White House as it is the wedding of Linda Johnson and Capt. Robb. The entire capital must be in quite a buzz.

Today is a day off, and I am feeling extra exhausted. Also, I have developed a peculiar gastro-intestinal disturbance. So, I caught up on my rest by sleeping until 1000 hrs. and did my semi-weekly wash of towels, uniforms and socks. Along with the chaplain, Eleanor Kutchoodon and Jim Manion, I spent a couple hours at the Division Library this afternoon. It's a quiet place and we all enjoyed the relaxation of the soft, padded lounge chairs.

As we were returning we were met by the company clerk saying, 'There have been some casualties', and we rushed to the E.R. to find three Vietnamese civilians with gunshot wounds, likely from the terrorist activity that never seems to stop around here. It does appear, sometimes, to be a story without an end.

Friday, 15 December, 1967: It is another chilly day. The radio says that it is 64° F, but I have been in plenty of weather that was 0° F or lower and it didn't seem as penetrating as this. It is due to the unrelenting dampness.

It was unusually quiet in the wards today, with the exception of one fellow who came in with a non-surgical leg injury. The truck he'd been riding in hit a land mine on the An Khe pass. We also got an inebriated GI with head lacerations. Later, we had a soldier with a severe fracture of his basal skull; he was in bad shape when he arrived, and we realized that he would have to be Med Evac'd to Qui Nhon. We started him on fluids and oxygen, and he appeared stabilized by the time he departed.

My headaches remain intense, and fortunately, I was able to sleep for a couple of hours this afternoon.

Wednesday, 20 December, 1967: At around 1110 hrs. a Med Evac chopper landed on the pad near the hospital, and one always wonders what it might be bringing us. In this case it was Colonel Boyson, the Commanding Officer of the 55th Medical Group, of which we are a part. Our scheduled nurses staff meeting was canceled because of his arrival, but we will meet tomorrow to learn the reason for his visit. There are more rumors that our unit will be disbanded after the first of the year, and of course, I am wondering where I will be assigned. Such uncertainly is not to my liking!

Eleanor Kutchoodon and I walked to the P-X this afternoon where I bought Kendall Haines his birthday gift—tomorrow is his day. Later, the NCOs had a Christmas party for the officers, and everyone had a splendid time. The steaks were extra-delicious, I thought, and there was eggnog—very luscious. It's been a long time since I had any, and it really hit the spot.

Thursday, 21 December, 1967: I awakened early by the sound of jets and large planes over head, and I am concerned. They are all heading north, and it means that there will be some activity on the DMZ today. The planes continued to pass overhead for an entire hour. I almost hate to see the so-called 'Christmas Truce' come, since I'm afraid that the action over that period may turn out to be greater than ever.

Friday, 22 December 1967: A beautiful sunny day; nothing out of the ordinary happened. We did an appendectomy and treated a soldier for salt and pepper fragment wounds—a claymore mine blasting cap had gone off near him.

I finally gave in and consulted the surgeons today, and the results were what I expected: A pilonidal cyst. I am hoping to avoid surgery, and promise to be faithful in taking Sitz baths in the hope that they will help.

The mail really came through today! I received two tapes from Ellen and a total of 35 letters from other folks. A real jackpot!

Saturday, 23 December, 1967: Yesterday was boom, today is bust for mail! President Johnson is in Cam Rhan Bay and planes were neither landing nor taking off.

Our officer's Christmas party was held this evening, and turnout was great, including officers from other units. We had grilled steak, ham and chicken, baked beans, potato salad ... and more eggnog!

Sunday, 24 December, 1967: A light sick call this morning. I went to chapel, which had a good attendance; the time is now 11:30 AM. Lou returned from Qui Nhon to report that the severely wounded fellow he accompanied there is doing remarkably well—much better than expected. He is apparently rational and has shown no evidence of heart damage. We are all thankful for the report.

We spent a busy afternoon welcoming dignitaries. General Telson, the 1st Cavalry C.O. was here along with the General of the entire II Corps of the Vietnamese Army. They toured the wards this afternoon, speaking to and distributing gifts to patients.

The choir met at 1900 hrs. and we caroled on the wards, then went for cookies and hot chocolate in the mess hall. After that, Al, Jim, the Chaplain, Maj. Ebert and I went to Eleanor's room, helped her decorate her tree and opened our gifts. It was a marvelous time. At 2300, the Episcopal services were held in the chapel. Between that service and midnight mass, the choir sang to a packed house—there wasn't even standing room.

Monday, 25 December, 1967: Christmas Day, 1967… in Vietnam! May it be a blessed and quiet day for everyone.

Yesterday, my day didn't end until 0200 hrs. and at present it is 0710. It is raining quite hard, but it looks as though it may clear off. There have only been two patients on sick call, so unless business suddenly picks up, it should be a quiet day all around.

Our bi-Faith service in the chapel at 1100 hrs. was well-attended and a real inspiration. I recorded it in its entirety, and will send it to Ellen— she can keep it for future reference.

Our traditional Christmas Day dinner was very nice: Roast turkey with all the trimmings.

In closing, I must say that this has been a beautiful and bright Christmas Day in the Central Highlands. A blessed one, even though I am not able to spend it with members of my family.

Sunday, 26 December, 1967: Last year at this time, I was preparing my annual Christmas letter from the Medical Field Service School at Ft. Sam Houston, Texas. Little did I realize that I would be writing this year's letter from a quonset hut in the Central Highlands of South Vietnam.

After completing six weeks of basic training in mid-December, 1966, I took several days leave and was afforded the opportunity to spend the Christmas season in Illinois and Iowa. During the time I was in Illinois I disposed of a great deal of my antique inventory accumulated over the years, listed our Quincy home for sale and spent the remainder of my time visiting friends and attending social functions with Ellen. We then accompanied my folks to Iowa, where we spent the remainder of my leave visiting the Colesburg and Manchester area.

On Christmas afternoon, Ellen boarded a bus from Cedar Rapids to return to Quincy and I boarded a United Airlines plane and returned to San Antonio. I am enjoying those happy memories as I spend this Christmas 12,000 miles from my loved ones.

In early January our home sold and we found our furniture en route to our new apartment on the Ft. Sam Houston military installation. Two days after it arrived, Ellen and my folks came down and soon we were all in the business of housekeeping once more. My folks spent the following two months with us, enjoying the mild winter weather of south-central Texas. During that time we visited Old Mexico, visited the citrus groves of the Rio Grande Valley and made numerous trips to sites of interest around the San Antonio area.

In mid-March, after the folks left, Ellen began working in the intensive care unit at the Nix Hospital in downtown San Antonio. She found it an interesting place to work. We spent until early June at Ft. Sam Houston where I was assigned as head nurse of one of the four orthopedic nursing units.

In June we found ourselves again packing and moving; this time, it was back to Quincy. During my 17 days of leave, we were busy getting Ellen settled in a comfortable apartment just a block and a half from Blessing Hospital where she is presently employed as the In-Service Education Coordinator. This position, along with her interest in sewing and other social activities should keep her quite busy.

On July 1st, I boarded a plane, and via Hawaii, Guam and the Philippines, I found myself, on July 5th, beginning my 365 day tour in the Republic of South Vietnam. My assignment is to a 100 bed medical clearing company, which is actually functioning as a station hospital. I am the Assistant Chief Nurse as well as being the supervisor of the emergency room and outpatient department. Additionally, I am the in-service education coordinator with the responsibility of planning and presenting in-service programs for the professional and ancillary personnel of the unit. These combined duties keep me busy most of the time.

Without a doubt, I have found Vietnam to be a land of more contrasts than any other place I have ever visited. It is a country of great poverty and people with poor educational backgrounds; medical facilities are all but non-existent, and those that are available are primitive. And yet, it is a land of extreme beauty, where the sunrises are more beautiful than any I have seen before—in part because it frequently rains while the sun is shining.

I cannot say that my experience in Vietnam has been unhappy, nor can I say that I will not be glad to leave this war-torn country.

I pray that this will be a joyous and blessed Holiday season for each of you and that we will share together the rewards of a new found peace among nations of the earth in this upcoming year.

Friday, 29 December, 1967: A bright, warm, beautiful morning. We had a big sick call for the first time since Christmas; afterwards, we took an in-service class on malaria.

Late this afternoon we received two ARVN soldiers with severe gunshot wounds. One had injuries to his lower jaw and we called in the oral surgeons from the dental detachment to care for him. The other had abdominal wounds and went immediately to surgery. We pumped blood into him, but it all poured out holes in his back immediately. The surgeons spent three hours trying to save him, but to no avail. He died after about three hours on the table.

I unwound in the evening with some plum pudding and hard sauce that Jim Manion's wife had sent; Jim steamed it on his hot plate, and it was excellent.

Saturday, 30 December, 1967: This afternoon we treated a fellow who had been brought in from a patrol on the Bong Son Plains where he had been shot at almost point blank range. He had severe arm injuries with nerve and artery damage; also, he had wounds to his spleen, pancreas, liver and stomach. He spent 7 ½ hours in the O.R. and received many pints of blood—currently, he is alive, but his condition is guarded.

Six of us went to the Can-Do Club in the evening, and at around 2000 hrs., there was an alert. During an alert you simply stay put, so we remained at the club until the alert was lifted at 2130 hrs.. When we returned to the O.R, we learned that eleven patients had been admitted while we were gone, but they had not been injured during combat. They were marching to the Green Line where they were going to help guard the perimeter and were struck by a truck that drove directly into their formation.

It is amazing the variety of ways that people wind up in the hospital over here.

Sunday, 31 December, 1967: A cloudy, damp, misty morning, nowhere near as nice as it has been. The fellow with the abdominal injuries that we treated yesterday is alert and doing surprisingly well—we transferred him to Qui Nhon as soon as he was stable enough to move. Time will tell...

At around 6:30 AM we got three fellows in who had been in a jeep accident; all had sizable scalp lacerations.

As soon as my shift is over, I intend to go to the New Year's Eve services at the chapel, then call it a day. Tomorrow begins a new year, and all of us in the war effort wonder what it will bring...

PART TWO

The Military Draft

Many of the early protests against the war in Vietnam centered on forced military conscription. As the war escalated under Johnson, more and more young people were sent to Vietnam under the threat of imprisonment, and by 1967—the era of this journal—nearly fifty percent of enlisted men in the army were draftees.

At the end of the war, it was estimated that about half of the combat deaths were conscripts.

At the time, many Americans considered the system of the draft, rather than the draft itself, the root of the unfairness. Undergraduates and, until 1968, graduate students could defer military service until they completed college. The National Guard and Army Reserves were options most often taken by middle and upper-class draftees, whereas less privileged youths served and died in Southeast Asia in disproportionate numbers. As a result, Vietnam was often referred to as a 'working-class war'.

In 1969, Nixon instituted a lottery system, attempting to make the draft seem more balanced and fair. In September 1971, Congress passed his proposal for an All-Volunteer Force, and in July 1973, Nixon terminated the draft.

In the end, of the 27 million men eligible for conscription, 8,720,000 enlisted (often to beat the draft and choose their branch of the military where they would serve), 2,215,000 were drafted.

Almost 16 million Vietnam era youths never served. Of that 16 million, 15,410,000 were deferred, exempted, or disqualified and an estimated 570,000 were draft offenders. Among them, over 209,517 were accused of draft violations.   8,750 were convicted, and 3,250 were imprisoned.

Monday, 1 January, 1968: A new year is upon us, and it is probably for the best that we don't know what it has in store for us. Last night, I went to the New Year's Eve Watch Night services at the chapel; it began at 10:30 PM. There was a half-hour movie, hot chocolate and at 11:30 we began our vesper service consisting of scripture, song, communion and silent prayer. Service closed at exactly midnight.

After a raucous New Year's Eve for many, I expected a lot more patients today, but ultimately, it was quite slow.

Wednesday, 3 January, 1968: Today is Mom's birthday—I hope she got my card! I was off today and accomplished very little other than sleeping and reading from my new antique's guidebook I got for Christmas. It was nice and sunny, and after I cleaned my room I washed my clothes. They dried quickly.

Thursday, 4 January, 1968: As quiet and uneventful as yesterday was, today was the opposite and will be long remembered.

At 0300 hrs. we were awakened by the most horrible explosion; Lou and

I were out the door within seconds. In the E.R., Sgt. Dunbar assured us that they were outgoing munitions. They continued for about twenty minutes, even after we had crawled back into bed, but at 0330, the sirens sounded, assuring us that it was the real thing and that there was enemy activity in the immediate area. We were up again at once and threw on our boots, uniforms and helmets and headed to the E.R. I was the first one to arrive—I don't have far to go.

The first thing we did was cover all the doors and windows with blankets so that we could use the lights if and when we received casualties. At the door, we looked to the sky, which was ablaze with flares—these lit up the ground so that the gunners could see 'Charlie' on the ground. The noise of battle continued for an hour and a half, and when it finished, we took in a single GI with fragment wounds to the arm. Amazingly, he was the only casualty. From him we learned that the heliport had been mortared and that an attempt had been made to knock out the control tower. Apparently, some of the Chinooks had been hit, and these cost $2 million each.

When all-clear sounded, a few of us went over to the heliport to see the damage for ourselves. Six Chinooks were damaged, though not too seriously. We could actually see the spots where the mortars hit the ground since the propulsion mechanisms buried themselves in the ground to a depth of about 8 inches, forming a 'post hole'. We were told that between 50 and 70 rounds were fired at us. And, by the looks of it, they had been creeping closer and closer to our hospital. I am convinced that we were saved by the gunships in the air during the attack; these big aircraft fire 500 rounds a minute and they must have absolutely disintegrated the Vietcong on the ground. This is the first time that this camp has been mortared since April.

Friday, 5 January, 1968: I was awaken at around 0430 hrs. by operating room personnel who came to get my roommate—it seemed that they had two Vietnamese patients brought in, one with an open compound hip fracture and the other with a traumatic amputation of the foot. Both required immediate surgery and both were the result of enemy hostility in An Khe during the time of our alert. Our main gate faces An Khe, and reports are that the Vietcong blew up the police station, and the ambulance driver that dropped off our two patients said that there were 'bodies laying all over downtown An Khe'.

He also stated that by now, about half of the remaining population had packed up and moved, but we have no idea where. All I can say is that if our troops are forced to shell the area due to Vietcong infiltration, they had better be far, far away.

We are grateful that there appear to have been no American casualties during the attack, but we have been warned about another potentially restless night, though we don't know the hour or the time. Oh, how I wish the whole business could be brought to a rapid conclusion.

Thursday, 6 January, 1968: Gratefully, there was no more enemy activity over the night. Even so, there were steady flares from our side, and I still didn't sleep as well as I would have liked.

Tomorrow we will start an experimental new shift, 8 hours per day, six days a week. I will be assigned to the Medical Ward, # 4, and I really enjoy it—it is a wonderful change of pace, and I am learning a lot about care of malaria patients.

We received two Vietnamese soldiers who had been injured between here and Pleiku; also, a G.I who had been attacked on the Pleiku road. Also, another one of those 'strange' cases: A mechanic who had gotten his head stuck between the vehicle frame and the tire while he was working on it. He had severe facial lacerations which extended to his inner ear and had to be evacuated to Qui Nhon.

There was a lot of firing on the perimeter today, lots of big weapons being fired; the flares were fired continuously, lighting up the sky. I was sure we would have an alert, but that never came.

Monday, 8 January, 1968: We did have a brief alert today, in the evening. It was followed by a tremendously loud noise with no firing afterward. It left me with a very peculiar feeling. I am not sure why.

Wednesday, 10 January, 1968: There was even more activity in downtown An Khe last night, with several civilians killed and quite a number of injured brought to our E.R. Three were operated on immediately, and one died just as the surgeons finished removing a lung. Two more had neurological injuries and had to be evacuated to Qui Nhon. The report is that the number of Vietcong in our area has increased dramatically in the past week and I fear for what might happen next.

I received a letter from Jerry Baumgartner today, perhaps the saddest letter I have ever gotten. He told me that on 22 December he had been diagnosed with a metastasized cancer of his lung to his left hip. He is taking more cobalt treatments, but I am convinced that his time is very limited and that I will never, ever see him again. He sent me photographs of his girls, and they are so beautiful, so precious. I know I must write to him, but I am at a total loss as to what to say. I am baffled. I wish there was something I could do for him, but what?

Saturday, 13 January, 1968: A slow day for patients, a busy day for dignitaries. Visiting our camp was Colonel Boyson, the Deputy Commander of the USARV, Lt. Col. Long from the 67th Evac. Hospital and the Commanding Officer of the 55th Medical Group, Col. Clifford, and Col. Jennie L. Caylor, Chief of Nursing in Vietnam. The purpose of their visit remains to be seen, but we are uneasy and uncertain what our future is.

Had a Vietnamese woman in who had been hit by a truck; she suffered a broken left arm and a fractured right femur. Surgery was considered, but it was decided that her condition was too grave to have her survive. When I went off duty, she was not doing well.

A quiet night, with very little firing on the green line; only a single flare was fired in the northeast. It kept me up until around 12:30 AM.

Sunday, 14 January, 1968: I had intended to sleep in due to the lateness of the hour I got to sleep, but at 0715 hrs. I was awakened by Spec. LaDoux who informed me that I was expected in the mess hall to have breakfast with the visiting Colonels. So, I quickly showered and dressed and reported as requested. After breakfast, I took Col. Caylor to review the wards, but she offered me no clue as to the reason behind the visit. And so, at 0900 hrs., we all remain desperately curious.

Monday, 15 January, 1968: It was a relatively quiet day, but one with something going on steadily. The surgeons operated on the Vietnamese lady who had been hit by a truck yesterday, then we took in a Vietnamese man who had picked up a grenade that then exploded and took off the tips of three of his fingers. After that, we received a G.I who had been shot near An Khe, where there is still a lot of hostile activity going on. He had a bullet wound to the face that penetrated his skull and basically destroyed his right eye—I sincerely doubt he will see out of it again. We did what we could for him, then evacuated him to Qui Nhon. Following him, we had another soldier that had been in a vehicle accident, although we don't know the entire extent of the circumstances.

My first day as acting chief nurse went pretty smoothly, without any major hurdles to address.

It is hot and sunny today, very pleasant. I had a tape from Carolyn who said that back in Iowa, it's 20° below zero!

Tuesday, 16 January, 1968: Another restless night with 175mm shells going off continually and echoing through the valley. We were roused at 0300 hrs. by the Executive Office Capt. McGarry who informed Lou that he was to be ready to move out within 24 hours, destination unknown. Then, in the morning, we received a call that said Lou needed to be packed and on the helipad within an hour, where a chopper would take him to Qui Nhon for further assignment. So we scurried and had him ready to go, but we are both curious as to where he will end up.

One of our enlisted men was ordered to Pleiku to be reassigned to a new unit yesterday, and he opted to go in an ambulance that was to accompany a convoy of trucks. He was boarded with all of his belonging when, for some reason, he decided to fly instead. Along the road to Pleiku the convoy was ambushed and the ambulance was completely destroyed. He lost his possessions, but these can be replaced. His life could not have been.

Amazing the role that fate constantly plays in our lives over here.

Thursday, 18 January, 1968: We received orders from the 55th Medical Group indicating that Lou and two male nurses were assigned to the 68th Medical Group headquartered in Long Binh, so he will end up down south somewhere, possibly the Delta area along the Cambodian border. It could be hot for him down there—in more ways than one.

Friday, 19 January, 1968: We took two fellows in this morning whose truck hit a roadside mine on the way to Pleiku, and then, a little after noon, we received eight Vietnamese who had been riding a bus that also hit a mine. It seems like Charlie is suddenly very, very busy.

Sunday, 21 January, 1968: Major Ebert was supposed to have returned yesterday; it is now 1700 hrs. and she has not arrived. I was supposed to be off today, but I was too busy with plans and actions to send more help to the green line, although I did get to church this morning and managed to get some letters answered.

This afternoon at around 1530 hrs., we received two soldiers whose gas truck had struck a mine—how it did not explode is a mystery. When we removed their boots, we actually poured gasoline out, and their clothing was saturated. They both required surgery.

8:00 PM: One of the men mentioned above has expired. He was given expert treatment and received 32 units of blood, but the internal bleeding he suffered just could not be controlled. It is one of those rare, but tragic instances where despite every effort, nothing could ultimately be done to save him.

There was considerable firing all through the night, and for the first time, flares over Hong Kong mountain just in back of our hospital. I am not sure what this means, but it can't be good.

Monday, January 22, 1968: Major Ebert still has not returned from leave, and we can't figure out what has happened to her.

Noise continues to pour in from the green line, and we learned that the 71st Evac Hospital was rendered completely useless from incoming rocket fire that knocked out their power and the underground water pipes burst. Also, they lost 95% of their medical supplies and two wards were completely destroyed. Only one patient, a Vietnamese civilian, was killed—fortunately, there had been enough time between the first shell and the second that the staff was able to evacuate the hospital.

Tuesday, January 23, 1968: Last night was again restless, since the steady fire of machine-guns makes sleeping difficult. It was a strange, rapid-paced day that began with a C-Section in the O.R. at 0700 hrs.

The Major finally returned from leave this evening, and was I ever glad to see her. Also, Jim Manion and Eleanor Kutchoodon both left for leave this morning. I had a call from Lou—it seems that he has been assigned to a newly-formed all-male unit, the 22nd Surgical Hospital. They are waiting to move out, but nobody knows exactly where.

Thursday, January 25, 1968: A relatively slow morning followed by an afternoon off—the Chaplain, his driver Lowell and I made an enjoyable trip to the green line, stopping at the ridge of Hong Kong mountain and climbing an observation tower where we had a marvelous view of all the surrounding terrain. Then we visited the area where they have set up the massive 175 mm self-propelled guns that are making all the noise every night. And no wonder—their barrels are 36 ft. long and the 125 lb. shells they fire have a range of 27 miles! Amazingly, the sergeant in charge said that they don't even use earplugs when they fire them.

A group of us played pinochle after dinner—a long game that lasted until 12:30 AM.

Friday, January 26, 1968: (find letter)

Sunday, January 28, 1968: Another short night as the sirens called us to alert at 0100 hrs., where we remained for 2 ½ hours. The report is that two Vietcong were killed on Hong Kong mountain after they had wired the ammunition dump for detonating. That would have rocked things around here.

Monday, 29 January, 1968: The Vietcong are definitely within the perimeter of our base camp—we had a fellow in the E.R. this morning who was hit by grenade fragments when he got up to use the latrine. It is impossible to forget how precarious our situation is here.

We are supposed to be on a truce for Vietnam's New Year, Tet. I wonder how long that will last?

Tuesday, 30 January, 1968: The Tet truce was called off at noon because of enemy violations, and an unusually large number of lives have been lost despite our efforts at a cease-fire.

Pleiku was mortared again last night, and there is street fighting in An Khe as well as Qui Nhon, where the Vietcong has taken over the radio station.

'Hell' has finally broken out, and it can't be long before we are hit here.

I retired at 2100 hrs., very apprehensive like everyone. We have been ordered to have our gas masks at our fingertips because if our perimeter is attacked, we intend to use gas.

Wednesday, 31 January, 1968: Well, we made it through the night without incident, and I was shocked when the alarm when off at 6:00 AM and found that everything had been quiet.

The 1st Platoon, representing about a third of our enlisted men, were placed on 72 hour alert, meaning they will likely be leaving soon.

I called the folks through the MARS station this evening, and it took an hour between the time the call was placed and the time I got through. I could barely hear them, but what I did hear made me feel extremely good.

Thursday, 1 February, 1968: Five months from today I will be homeward bound!

Late last night, we received two GIs; one required an exploratory laparotomy, the other a gastrostomy and the amputation of his left foot. Both seem to be doing okay.

Awakened at midnight by a tremendous amount of noise from a series of artillery all being fired at once, and we certainly expected that an alert would follow, but there was none.

Friday, 2 February, 1968: I worked on Ward #1 today—the Intensive Care Unit. It is air conditioned, so I didn't mind the intense heat so much, although it really hits you when you go outside. One of my patients was a truly pitiful case, and I had to sit by his bedside for most of the day; he needed that much reassurance. He'd been in for about 36 hours, the victim of hostile fire—both eyes were bandaged and I'm told that he will lose sight in one of them. One arm and both legs were heavily dressed and one of his feet had been amputated. Not only that, but his abdomen had been operated on, so his entire mid-section was bandaged, too. He'd had a gastrostomy, and had a tube protruding from his mouth for drainage. He could take nothing orally, and spent a lot of time begging for water and did not seem completely rational, so it was impossible to explain the situation to him, only listen to his pleading, over and over. At times he would cling to me, then slip into a restless sleep while he repeated, 'I did the best I could... I never liked the Army, but I made up my mind to make the most of it...' His name was Ernie and he was from just south of Salt Lake City.

Off duty, I found an uneasy quietness around camp. Today's Pacific Stars & Stripes carried a detailed report of the incredible enemy attacks all across the country, leaving thousands and thousands of Vietcong dead. They even attacked the embassy in Saigon. You would think that they'd learn that they cannot win this war, but to them, apparently, the loss of life means little.

Saturday, 3 February, 1968: We took in among the most nightmarish injuries today—five GIs with punji stake wounds. The group had been dropped in a landing zone covered with tall elephant grass, and evidently the V.C. had planted the stakes there. These sharpened sticks are often purposely contaminated with pig feces to induce infections.

A severely wounded Vietcong soldier was brought to E.R. a little after midnight; prior to his capture, they had shot and killed the soldier that was with him. The one that survived had gunshot wounds to the nose and face and had lost an eye. Our intelligence people questioned him for two hours before taking him to surgery, and apparently were able to elicit a lot of useful but disturbing information: Apparently, there are still many, many Vietcong in the area.

Tuesday, 6 February, 1968: Even though it was late when we finished playing cards last night, I couldn't sleep, so I decided to try out my new typewriter and write some letters. At around 0100 hrs. I heard a series of loud, unusual noises unlike anything I've heard before. I suspected that it might be incoming mortar rounds, and it turned out that I was right—the alert sirens soon went off. We were at it again.

I headed for the hospital where we soon began receiving casualties. Mortars had been aimed at two different spots across the post, both the barracks of enlisted men. In all, we took in 25 wounded men, some in very serious condition. At least one was put on I.V.s and classified as 'expectant', which meant that he was not expected to live. However, with the doctor's diligence, he was finally taken to the operating room where he not only survived surgery, but seems to be doing much better.

We received a single KIA (Killed In Action), a very young man who had a small wound on his neck, but nothing more. There wasn't a trace of blood. Apparently he had been struck by shrapnel in precisely the wrong spot, a vital neck artery, and bled to death internally. He was still warm and his face showed no expression whatsoever—how very tragic it is.

The alert was called off at 0400 hrs., but we were cautioned to sleep with fatigues on and helmets ready. Needless to say, I hardly slept a wink.

Wednesday, 7 February, 1968: At around 0200 hrs. we received a GI who had been shot in the head while patrolling the green line. Two hours later, we began to hear a tremendous amount of activity in the underbrush of the ravine behind our barracks, at the base of Hong Kong mountain. Soon, a gun ship with searchlights began hovering over the area, and it was soon followed by the sound of gunfire.

I was left with a tremendous headache, and wound up writing a letter to the editor of our local paper—I wonder if they will actually print it.

(Appeared in 'The Manchester Press' and several other newspapers in February, 1968)

Dear Editor,

After 7 months in Vietnam, I wonder if each of your readers is as aware of this war that is going on over here as I am.

As a registered nurse and a member of the Army Nurse Corps, I have to see the worst aspects of it. I am referring to those of severe physical injury, mental anxiety and disturbance, prolonged suffering and more often than I like to admit—death.

I wish that I did not have to witness these things. I would prefer the insulation of seeing and hearing only statistical reports and newspaper headline about offensives, skirmishes, assaults and body counts.

Instead, for me and many more thousands like me, the war is now a long and terrible list of individual tragedies reaching into the several hundreds. The impact of the situation we are in cannot escape me and I sincerely hope that a personal communication from me will make a lasting impression of the gravity of this situation to each of you at home.

As the economists reassure us, it may be fiscally possible to cope with a war on poverty, race problems, continued urban development, crime, and others along with the real war that is going on, but I assure you that it is not emotionally possible for those who are here fighting it.

With continuing outbreaks such as we are witnessing, it won't be long before an impact of terribleness, futility and personal involvement will hit every American citizen, no matter how oblivious of the present situation he may now be.

Despite sporadic demonstrations, both pro and con, about this war, it seems apparent that complacency and a spirit of procrastination still prevails.

I can assure the reader that one day at our hospital would make a true believer out of anyone. Please give Vietnam your individual attention and make a conscious effort to support and encourage all reasonable approaches for people at home to terminate this situation we are in. It is a very small sacrifice that each of you can make.

- Capt. Fredrick O. Phelps

Thursday, 8 February, 1968: Saying some farewells to friends and colleagues these days: Al Podgorny is packed and sent his hold baggage today. He leaves in two weeks. Harold Chase left for home the day before yesterday. Otherwise, today wound up being quite uneventful.

Saturday, 10 February, 1968: This was my first swing at the night shift, and it's now a little past 0130 hrs. It's relatively quiet—we have five patients on Ward #1. I just changed a colostomy bag on a young Vietnamese boy who had been struck with grenade fragments; also, a Vietnamese man who had been shot on the left side of his face. The bullet entered his ear and exited his nose, tearing out everything between the two points. He's attached to an I.V., underwent a tracheotomy and has a catheter, and seems to be doing well.

We have been on standby alert since coming on shift at 1:00 PM, and we have been warned to be combat ready at all times—those on duty to have field gear and those off duty to sleep in fatigues. The intelligence people have informed us that there is a large group of enemy forces near the perimeter. We hear the large guns being fired, but so far, nothing else.

Wednesday, 14 February, 1968: Happy Valentine's Day! It has been remarkably quiet tonight—quite a change from the steady firing we have heard all week. The wards are quiet as well; I have really struck it lucky during these night shifts, and I hope it hold out as I have two more to go.

Thursday, 15 February, 1968: Well, luck certainly ran out; this has been the busiest night since I went on the late shift. Among the non-stop activity was the soldier who had the chest tube and bleeding stress ulcer grew rapidly worse and required constant attention; vital signs were taken every half hour, and he received so many pints of blood, but he kept vomiting up blood even so. I did not think we could pull him through the night, but somehow, we managed to do so.

Friday, 16 February, 1968: Well, this shift certainly started out as hectic as last night. As I came on duty, the 3 – 11 nurse informed me that the young Vietnamese child who had been admitted this afternoon did not make it; we had worked frantically over him but to no avail. 'John Doe', the GI who had gastric surgery during the day seemed to have a pretty good night; I honestly did not expect to come on duty and find him alive.

We had another patient who'd had an exploratory laparotomy yesterday afternoon. He had been in a convoy heading toward Pleiku when he was ambushed; the saddest part is that he was scheduled to leave for home in two days.

A Montagnard woman in an advanced state of pregnancy was admitted, due at any time. I'm not real well versed in midwifery and prayed that she wouldn't deliver on my shift. She did not. Whew!

At around 1:30 AM, just as things started to settle down, we received a call about another ambush and were told to prepare for five incoming patients to be delivered by 'dust-off' helicopter. Within fifteen minutes they arrived, the most seriously wounded being a litter patient with a gunshot wound to the left eye—I have no doubt that the eyesight is gone. The other four were less seriously wounded, and one was released. This activity lasted until about 0300 hrs., then things really did quiet down and I was able to get some letters written and a tape off to Ellen.

Monday, 19 February, 1968: I managed to sleep until 11:00 AM—I must have been more tired than I thought. After breakfast I went to the P-X and ordered some material; three pieces for sports coats for myself—one of grey striped flannel, one of lightweight dark blue with a subdued plaid design and the third of gorgeous, navy blue cashmere. I also ordered a piece of black and olive strip for Ellen to make a suit. The whole order came to $55.00. I couldn't get a cashmere sports coat alone for that in the States.

Tuesday, 20 February, 1968: A bit quieter this evening than yesterday, but we still ended up taking in five GIs who had been in a truck accident.

One was dead on arrival, one was Med Evac'd to Qui Nhon for a basal skull fracture and the other three have been kept for observation.

At half past midnight, we took in two fellows from an armored personnel carrier, which had gone over an embankment, but they were not as badly injured as we had been led to believe.

At 0130 hrs. we received a man who was having an acute psychotic episode. He was hallucinating and we had to administer Thorazine to get him calm enough to sleep. Things were quiet from then on, and I spent my time 'spoiling' the little Vietnamese baby delivered yesterday.

The sun came up, and I must mention that it is one of the most beautiful dawns I have ever seen. Camp Radcliffe in the foreground, and behind it, the outline of the mountains as they projected into the sky; from behind this silhouette, the sun rose, spreading a brilliant array of all the shades of red, fuchsias, oranges, roses, gold and yellow. This then faded to the bright blue of morning. It is a shame that these things don't last longer, and even worse that the people in camp, who see so much that is ugly, don't take more time to appreciate some of the simple beauties around them.

Wednesday, 21 February, 1968: In my mail today was a letter from a Mrs. Andrew Johnson of Fredericksburg and a Mr. Kenneth Pilgrim of Independence who had seen my letter-to-the-editor in the Des Moines Register and the Waterloo Daily Courier, respectively. Liz Moser also mentioned that she had read it in the Telegraph Herald. I am most interested to find out what other responses it will bring.

It has been very, very quiet outside tonight, and it is hard not to be a little uneasy. The uncertainty of the future can be very stressful.

We did take in three young Vietnamese children needing immediate surgery; they had found a live grenade by the river and apparently pulled the pin. By the time I left my shift, they were all doing well.

Saturday, 24 February, 1968: A fairly uneventful day, and I had a chance to catch up on some correspondence. Carolyn enclosed an article from the Cedar Rapids Gazette that had printed one of my letters home and even included a picture of me—not a very good one, though.

I also heard from Jerry Baumgartner's wife who reports that he has been in the University Hospital since February 5th on heavy pain medications. My hopes are fading for ever seeing him alive again.

Sunday, 25 February, 1968: After chapel this evening, I walked over to the nurses quarters and met with Lt. Kutchoodon and Maj. Moore; we had a general gripe session over the way things have been going lately. There seems to be a lack of firm direction on the part of the ranking officers in this unit and we feel it is simply apathy. We all agreed that we'd feel better if the unit was more regimental and we knew where we stood. Part of the problem is probably the news we received earlier— that the 616th Medical Co. Clearing would be disbanded in the near future and that this facility would be taken over by the 17th Field Hospital. It is completely unclear what will happen to us. The enlisted men will likely be divided into platoons and be sent toward the DMZ as medical support for the combat troops. The professional compliment of doctors and nurses may remain here and become a part of the 17th Field Hospital. Or maybe not—the point is, we just don't know. Also, we have been told that our Commanding Officer, who has only been here a short while, will be soon reassigned; whoever replaces him will be our fourth C.O. since I arrived.

All this combined probably plays an important role in the disruption of the attempts of key people to control subordinate officers and enlisted men. The intake of alcoholic beverages by some seems to have been increasing lately, and to the rest of us, this is disturbing indeed. I don't mean to sound Puritanical in the least, but drinking certainly affects their ability to diagnose accurately and contribute effectively.

Monday, 26 February, 1968: A little past midnight, we received a young soldier who was suffering from an acute situational reaction; his 1st

Sergeant reports that he'd only been with the unit for a week and his former unit had been nearly wiped out in an enemy ambush. I have no doubt that this contributes to his present mental state. He was given a Thorazine injection and has been sleeping quietly in Ward #1 ever since.

Thursday, 29 February, 1968: February 29th—a day that will not occur again for a while! It has no particular significance to me except that it means I will have to stay in Vietnam for an extra day, and as precarious as things are, that could be important.

Friday, 1 March, 1968: This marks the eighth month I have been in this strange, far-off land called Vietnam, having left friends and family behind to serve my country. Well, it is not so strange or far away to me now. I feel that I have developed a great deal of insight into the needs of Vietnam and her people; I can't say that I have done a great deal to solve political problems, but I do like to think that I have done something to help ease the pain of the native people. And, in some small away, helped America and the men who are fighting over here in what is legally called a 'conflict', but what seems like a war in every sense of the word.

In four months, I will be putting both my feet back on the soil of the good old U.S.A., and what a grand feeling that will be!

Saturday, 2 March, 1968: I am sorry to say that our luck in not receiving casualties ran out at 0130 hrs. this morning when a helicopter delivered two GIs. One had been killed in action and was D.O.A.; the other had fragment wounds, but was not seriously hurt—although he was, understandably, quite shook up. Apparently both men had been sleeping when a grenade was tossed through an opening in their bunker and exploded near where the dead fellow lay. He took the full brunt of it—a small shelf separated him from his companion, but that was enough to save the second man's life.

Monday, 4 March, 1968: I was awakened at 0100 hrs. with an order to report to the E.R. where a woman had been admitted who was about to deliver a baby. At the same time, we were told to expect two field casualties. The woman ended up delivering a still-born baby on the litter. The dead child looked perfectly healthy, but the infant mortality rate here is staggering.

We no sooner had her in Ward #1 when mortars began landing inside the base camp, sounding very close indeed. And shortly, instead of the two casualties we had expected, we received 27 wounded GIs and three Vietnamese patients—the largest number of injured I have seen at one time since arriving.

Shortly after getting this large group stabilized, we received five K.I.A.; two Vietnamese and three GIs. Apparently, one of the observation towers had been struck with a mortar and completely destroyed.

Of the first group, the most seriously injured was a young American soldier who had a bilateral sucking chest wound, a gunshot wound to his back that exited in the front; also, ten other bullet wounds to his hands, arms and legs. I was able to get chest tubes and I.V.s started, then he was taken to the O.R. Amazingly, he survived surgery and is listed as serious, but satisfactory.

Another GI had taken a bullet to his spinal cord and will be paralyzed for the rest of his life.

The rest were riddled with fragment wounds covering every conceivable part of their bodies. We ended up evacuating twelve of them to Qui Nhon.

Several of the fellows injured had only been in Vietnam for one day, and this was their first night here. Not a particularly warm welcome. A few more were short-timers with only a few days left on their tours of duty. Either scenario seemed to make the situation even worse.

Our Commanding Officer gathered us together in the afternoon and informed us that we could consider this 'just the beginning', and that we were to expect more activity—likely severe—during the night. Supposedly, several platoons of Vietcong are reported to be moving through the area, and ground fire between here and Pleiku is heavy.

On a less serious note, I got a new roommate this afternoon, Captain Gene Wedge, a nurse anesthetist who had been in the Marine Corps for eleven years before meeting his wife, a nurse, and leaving the Corps to attend nursing school. He's on his way to Qui Nhon, and will only be with us for about four days.

Tuesday, 5 March, 1968: Artillery fire fell strangely silent at around 10:00 PM, and the hospital is also quiet—I have been on duty two hours.

We did receive three patients—one a Vietnamese man who had a leg blown off and who went to surgery at once and seems to be doing well. The other two were American soldiers with the 589th Engineering Company; they had been in bed when hit. The least seriously wounded of the two was covered with fragment wounds over his back, had a broken fibula and a number of broken fingers. The other fellow is covered in bandages from his forehead to his feet, with injuries too extensive to describe, but include a fractured left ulna, fragment wounds to the right shoulder, lower back, left arm and right leg. He has chest tubes, a gastrostomy tube suctioning and an indwelling catheter. Remarkably, he seems to be doing quite well, and we visited for a while at midnight when I turned him. Like so many injured GIs we received, he was more concerned about his fellow soldiers than himself, and asked about several of them by name. Also, he worried about his mother's reaction when she is told of his injuries, saying that she had suffered a stroke in the past and had high blood pressure. I could only reassure him by telling him that she would receive continuing reports about his condition. He'd been in country for a year, and worried that his wounds might force him to leave the service.

He wanted to talk, so I sat at his bedside and listened. During the mortar attack, he told me, he had been in bed when first hit, then, attempting to get up, he was hit again and had to crawl to the NCO barracks. He told me that he had done a lot of praying on that crawl, especially that he did not lose consciousness, because he knew that if he did, he would not again awaken. Tears came to his eyes, and I understood that talking about the horror of his experience was good for him. He needed a listener, and I was happy to oblige.

Such are the experiences of an active duty nurse in a small hospital in the Central Highlands of Vietnam. And I assume that this is typical of many, many such stories that are going on currently at countless locations throughout the entire war zone.

Wednesday, 6 March, 1968: A fairly quiet night, but we did have a death on Ward #1 at about 0200 hrs.—an elderly Vietnamese woman who had been admitted with five others from her village, all of whom had been attacked during the night by Vietcong or N.V.A. The others, all children, including a three-year-old girl who now has a chest tube are doing well.

Tuesday, 12 March, 1968: A quiet day without much activity beyond a Vietnamese soldier who was shot in the abdomen on the streets on An Khe; he had an injury to the bladder which was repaired in surgery and inserted a supra-pubic tube and various I.V.s, and he seems to be doing well.

I didn't sleep too well; my sleeping pill acted up mid-morning and at noon, they woke me up to change the old mattresses in Ward #5 to some new ones that had arrived. I expect that tonight will be a long one.

Thursday, 14 March, 1968: Three patients in Intensive Care, one of them the A.R.V.N. (Army of the Republic of Vietnam) soldier who was injured yesterday, two others small Vietnamese children. One was a boy who had received some rather severe burns when a lantern in his home fell over; his face is edematous to the point where he can't open his eyes. The other is a two-year-old who was riding on a bus when it struck a landmine; he has a closed fracture of the left femur.

Both papasans (fathers) are staying with them. They hover over them constantly and seem very sincere.

One of the things about the Vietnamese family unit that I have seen is how closely knit they are. Also, it is unusual for me to see the male figure in the family take such a leading role in the care of small children, in almost complete contrast to the American culture.

Saturday, 16 March, 1968: A busy, busy night. Both of the Vietnamese children required vascular surgery, and one had a femoral artery craft; the other had a right radial artery reconstruction. Both, of course, required frequent checks of their vital signs throughout the night. We had eight patients that needed I.V.s and nearly all of our wards were filled.

It is not just us. We heard that Qui Nhon received 114 surgery patients yesterday. I can't imagine how tough a job they must have.

The young Vietnamese boy with the previous surgery and colostomy bag had to be readmitted for more surgery—they found further abscesses and adhesions. Sad to report that he is not doing very well.

I did manage to call my folks, and even though it is a day earlier at home, I knew that they would enjoy the call—it's Dad's 61st birthday.

Sunday, 17 March, 1968: The condition of our young Vietnamese patient continues to deteriorate despite all efforts. I am afraid that we will not be able to pull him through this time—he is so pale and thin, and his will to fight back is fading.

Monday, 18 March, 1968: Better news for the Vietnamese boy. He returned to surgery today and came out in pretty good shape. I guess it is just a matter of time and faith.

We also had an unusual case: A young Vietnamese girl came in with a 5 dong coin lodged in her esophagus. When it failed to dislodge by itself, surgeons took her to O.R. where they managed to dislodge it.

It has been awfully hot. The forecast predicted 95° F and it was every bit of that, if not more.

Friday, 22 March, 1968: About 50 enlisted men arrived today from the 17th Field Hospital, bringing our total up a considerable number. It seems likely that a number of the 616th people will be moving out before much longer, and plenty of these I will hate to see go since we really have been a pretty good group here. But, life in the Army is full of changes and I am wondering what will happen next. I am hoping to hear from the folks tomorrow.

Tuesday, 26 March, 1968: We had a sergeant brought in last night with a broken ankle and the D.T.s (delerium tremens caused by alcohol intake)! He had a restful night.

I received something from a papasan in a nearby village that I have waited a long time for. It is a woven piece of Montagnard fabric for which I had paid 400 piasters—about $3.50. Unfortunately, it smelled so bad I had to wash it in cold water; this morning I found that it had faded somewhat, but not so much as if I had used detergent, and I am still very pleased with it. The six-year-old son of the man that brought it to me had been admitted to the hospital for severe dehydration earlier; that is how I met him.

We had two stillborn births today; also, a Montagnard with a gunshot wound to the left thigh, and a GI with a punji stick wound.

A busy day, but it was made somewhat easier by our first choir practice this evening in preparation for our Easter sunrise service, and plenty of mail, including a tape from Ellen, letters from Aunt Opal, Carolyn, Kenneth Pilgrim, and my $100 bonus from the State of Illinois for serving in Vietnam. I wonder what special 'thing' I am going to spend it on!

Wednesday, 27 March, 1968: Some very big, very distressing news today. We admitted five Vietnamese civilians who were diagnosed with the plague. Supposedly, there is an epidemic in a nearby village. Fortunately, in modern times it is treatable. They were given I.V. fluids and antibiotics.

Later, a few of us decided to show slides in the chapel. I was pleased that this is the first time that some of mine were projected.

Saturday, 30 March, 1968: A day off today, and pay day as well—managed to get a few packages of miscellaneous items off to the folks; mostly things I wanted to be sure were waiting for me when I get home. Then, on to the PX, where the material I sent for had arrived—all except the navy blue cashmere.

Monday, 1 April, 1968: Today we became the 17th Field Hospital, and held a medical corps nurse and clinical tech meeting in the evening to cover new procedures to be followed and forms that needed to be completed for admission and discharge of patients.

We also heard that President Johnson announced that he would not seek re-election in the fall. At the same time, he announced a complete cessation of all bombing in North Vietnam. I am wondering what effect this will have on the war's progress. Personally, I am not in favor of trusting the North Vietnamese, but I guess time will tell.

'I Shall Not Seek, And I Will Not Accept, The Nomination Of My Party For Another Term As Your President...'

On March 31, 1968—two months after the infamous 'Tet Offensive'—Lyndon B. Johnson, 36th President of the United States, delivered the above, earth-shattering pronouncement during a national address.

The war in Vietnam was the central reason for his monumentous decision not to seek a second term.

Regarding Vietnam, Johnson made several strategic policy blunders during the course of his term in office, beginning with his decision to undersell the war to the American public while secretly escalating it. His reasoning was understandable, if essentially flawed: He believed that by rallying widespread public support for the war, the American public might demand a full-scale military response to the communist threat, up to and including the use tactical nuclear weapons. Johnson rightly believed that such action would lead to the involvement of the Russians and Chinese and result in a third World War.

However, as the truth of the 'secret war' leaked gradually to the American public, an overwhelming sense of having been deceived by the government settled over the nation's population, particularly among young people who felt somewhat disaffected by White House policies to begin with. Beginning in 1966, through demonstrations, petitions and various forms of civil disobedience, protests against these policies grew, likely culminating in the Pentagon Siege of October 21-22, 1967 during which 35,000 anti-war protesters descended on Washington to demand an end to the war.

Facing a serious challenge for the Democratic Party Presidential nomination for the Presidency by Senators Eugene McCarthy and Robert F. Kennedy, both of whom were campaigning on an anti-war platform, and exhausted Johnson tossed in the towel.

That decision, and the subsequent changes in national policy by Richard M. Nixon, altered world history in ways that are both subtle and momentous.

Tuesday, 2 April, 1968: Well, I was hoping for a quiet night at work, but that did not happen. Among our patients was a suspected VC who had received a gunshot wound to the larynx; they had to do a tracheotomy on him during surgery. Following this was the admittance of a GI with gunshot wounds to both thighs—the result of an accident. All the wards are full, and while we were preparing 29 patients for evacuation in the morning, at around 9:30 PM, mortar rounds began coming into the post, mostly landing near the 1st Cavalry R & R processing building, which is not very far from the hospital. This is the first of such activity we have had in a month. As a result of the shelling, we received 21 patients, three of whom required surgery. The rest were kept in the bunker until the all-clear siren sounded.

Thursday, 4 April, 1968: The hospital was quiet until about 5:00 AM; then we received a group of Montagnard soldiers who had been in a truck accident. Seven of them required surgery. After that, two GIs were brought in with fragment wounds received while manning guard posts just outside An Khe, one requiring abdominal surgery. We had seven I.V.s going at one time.

That means that our wards are nearly full again, and I don't know where we will put any new patients without an evac soon.

Saturday, 6 April, 1968: Again, things began slowly and I was able to write and read some letters. The last one I read was from Tom Wheeler, who told me that he had just received a three year assignment in Hawaii. How lucky can some people get!

At around 5:30 AM, one of the Montagnard soldiers (MIKE Forces) began to go bad on us. We started resuscitation measures and when I felt that his condition was worsening, called the doctor. Even so, he was pronounced dead an hour later. Apparently, he had a pulmonary embolus.

Sunday, 7 April, 1968: Palm Sunday, 1968.

A busy night on the ward, beginning at 12:30 AM when we received a Vietnamese civilian who had been hit by a truck and had internal injuries including a fractured urethra; he kept us busy all night giving him blood, oxygen, medications, taking various pressures, etc. But, we pulled him through the night.

Then we had a little boy who had been tending cattle and came across an M-79 grenade that went off, injuring both of his shoulders and thighs. Surgeons performed a femoral artery graft on his left leg and he seems to be doing fine.

Wednesday, 10 April, 1968: After a couple of quiet nights, tonight was the busiest one I have known since being in Vietnam. The onslaught of patients began fairly early in my shift; a helicopter was shot down between here and Pleiku and three casualties were brought in, one of whom had been killed in action. Another had a bullet wound in his knee; the other, severe facial injuries.

Then, we began receiving casualties from a series of ambushes, and after that, nine dead Vietcong soldiers who had been using a civilian bus for cover. The bus had been destroyed, and unfortunately, there were eight civilians aboard also. In all, the day saw over forty casualties from this activity, and of the 25 admitted, 12 had to be evacuated to An Khe. The O.R. crew were busy from 0900 hrs. to about 2300 hrs. and a lot of the cases were very serious; bowel resections, grafts, etc.

Friday, 12 April, 1968: We had a Good Friday service in the chapel this evening—it was very nice and the Communion service was particularly impressive. It had been a dark, dreary afternoon, and I note that it seems like Good Friday always is. But I had wondered what the weather would be like on this side of the world. To me, I find this to be a strange phenomenon which would be difficult for anyone to explain.

The wards remain busy, with seven I.V.s going, along with four nasogastric tubes, two tracheotomies, a newborn delivered by C-section and an older Vietnamese woman who was hit by a truck and suffered brain damage. She is not doing well.

Saturday, 13 April, 1968: Another beautiful, clear night in a huge valley in the Central Highlands of Vietnam; although our surroundings are not, perhaps, exactly as we would want them to be, I am sure that it would be difficult to find a lovelier place on the face of the earth. The sky is bright and beautiful as the moon wends its way across the sky, without a cloud to interrupt the progress of the great fluorescent ball.

Recently, there have been several flares in the sky over Sniper Hill, but none tonight.

Sunday, 14 April, 1968: Easter Sunday, 1968. I am reminded of Easters past, and all the pleasant experiences I had as a youth; the sunrise services sponsored by youth organizations followed by an Easter breakfast in the basement of the church which was conducted by the young people themselves. And, Easter dinner, with the traditional pineapple roll that Mom always bakes to perfection, then covers with a light glaze of powdered sugar frosting topped with diced maraschino cherries and chopped walnuts. Last Easter, we were in San Antonio, and I remember taking Ellen to work in the morning, then returning home to begin preparing Easter supper. I made a ham, which was pretty good if I say so myself.

It was slow on the ward, with the exception of one corpsman who gave me some trouble—he had been drinking on duty.

Monday, 15 April, 1968: The night began busy and remained so throughout. It started with a Montagnard soldier with a traumatic amputation of two fingers of the left hand. Later in the evening, we received two GIs with fragment wounds; one was dead on arrival, the other had neck wounds and a severing of the subclavian circulatory system. Doctors performed a tracheotomy and a thoracotomy; he was in the O.R. for 5 ½ hours, but when he returned from the operating room at around 4:30 AM, he was attached to two I.V.s of blood, a Bennett respirator, a catheter, a chest tube and a Gomco Suction pump. He has bright red hair and seems to be doing well.

At the same time as this fellow came in, we took in a GI with a ruptured appendix; we had to keep him in the ward until the surgeons finished up.

A busy night in the hospital, but outside, a beautiful and quiet one.

Tuesday, 16 April, 1968: Jim Manion received his port call today; he leaves on Friday. I shall surely hate to see him go, as he and Capt. Eleanor Kutchoodon are the only two officers left who were here when I arrived. Jim has been a particularly good friend to me through these long months since I arrived and I will miss him greatly.

Went to work at 10:30 AM and found that nine of 11 beds on Ward #1 were filled. Terry Lea, the soldier who had the neck surgery yesterday is doing well. He has had no respiratory distress and his color is good. Seeing these sorts of miraculous sights is a rewarding and gratifying experience, especially since he is so grateful and cooperative. We all hope he gets along fine.

We lost a 17 day old baby, however—he had been admitted with severe dehydration, and I knew when I first saw him that he would not live long. Why an infant should die of dehydration is a puzzle to me; the mother had access to milk and water, and she looks clean and well-kept. The baby was rumored to have been fathered by a GI, which is not uncommon over here.

We are also treating a year-old child with a cellulitis and necrosis of a place on his head where we removed an abscess about a week ago. I looks terrible. Of the nine patients we have on the ward, all of them have I.V.s going.

Saturday, 20 April, 1968: Up by 0700 hrs. today, and it is a bright and sunny morning. I saw Jim off an hour later, and there is a huge void in my life. First Harold, then Al, and now Jim. What great friends we have all been.

I tried to call Ellen during the night; the call went through almost immediately... and she was not home!

Five of us climbed Hong Kong mountain today. That may be an insignificant sentence, but it sure wasn't an insignificant journey! Up a steep and narrow path, through dense elephant grass, then up the rugged road that has recently been carved out of rugged terrain where the dust was so thick it was ankle deep. It took us an hour and a half to reach the top, and how hot and tired we were by then. I had attempted this same trip last year and could not quite reach the summit, but now that I have completed it, I was so impressed by the view. If it were not for the mountains in between, one could see all the way to Pleiku, 45 miles away. From base to summit, Hong Kong mountain is 2,360 feet, so now I consider myself a real mountain climber. The mountains themselves are beautiful as they blend into the blue-gray sky far off.

A difficult trip, but a rewarding one—I had a definite feeling of tachycardia near the top, but it was worth it. We returned to base for a rest and a shower a little after noon.

Thursday, 25 April, 1968: The red-haired patient with the severe neck wounds—the result of a Claymore mine explosion—was evacuated this morning. He had been doing poorly, but now is much improved. Before going off duty I prepared him and his belongings for his journey; I even used a felt marking pencil to make a black bow tie on his neck wound dressing! He got a kick out of that.

He asked about a camera that he had among his possessions and I assured him that I had packed it in his duty bag along with his other things. He told me that he wanted to make sure not to lose it as it had belonged to a close friend of his that had been killed. I learned further that he and his buddy were both from Houston, Texas, and that he intended to fly to Illinois, where his buddy's wife lived, to give her the camera. When I asked him where she lived in Illinois, he answered 'Liberty' and I just about fell over—that's only 14 miles from Quincy. Her name is Shirley Parliament, and I must find out if the folks around there know her. What a small world it seems to be!

Saturday, 27 April, 1968: Around 2:00 AM, while at work, I began to feel sick to my stomach, with the chills, dizziness, etc. Since it was slow I decided to come to my room and lie down; I wound up sleeping until 4:00 PM! I have no idea what the problem was, but I felt fine when I got up.

Tuesday, 30 April, 1968: Twins were delivered by C-section today. The mother was eclamptic and had convulsed about an hour earlier, but fortunately, everything went well and the two little ones are doing fine.

Wednesday, 1 May, 1968: Two months to the day and I should be very near home! These words sound very pleasant to me indeed!

Glad to report that the twins are doing well; they slept through the night, waking only to have their diapers changed. They are so cute. Their mother is doing fairly well also.

Saturday, 4 May, 1968: A busy, busy night. It began with a Vietnamese man we suspected of having meningitis and placed in isolation; then, a GI named John who we received last week with severe injuries from a rocket attack went bad. His blood pressure suddenly dropped, his pulse began to race, his respiration fell to almost zero. We took vital signs every fifteen minutes, but his condition did not improve. Despite having worked with him diligently and steadily since his surgery, he finally expired at 9:20 AM. It was quite hard for all of us to take.

Sunday, 5 May, 1968: It's a few minutes past three in the morning and the hospital is quiet, so I will take a few minutes to write. I have just finished my regular ward rounds, I have redone the emergency drug cart in the Intensive Care Unit and just prior to beginning this journal entry, helped with the feeding of the twins delivered here a little over a week ago. They have had their diapers changed, their bottoms powdered and their stomachs refilled, so they ought to be comfortable for the next few hours. They are really precious little ones and the best natured little things. I suppose they know they had better be with nine more children at home. And, what a place to have to grow up. I suppose it is a blessing that they really don't know what lies ahead.

At eight this morning I heard helicopters leaving the helipad and when I went to the Admissions and Dispositions office to inquire as to the reason, I was told that one of the checkpoints just beyond our perimeter had been overrun by Vietcong, and that we would be getting several casualties. Well, we got them all right. Two were dead on arrival and there were about eight others with terrible, terrible injuries. One had both legs blown off at the mid-thigh; he was also missing half his face, and air bubbled out beneath his eye every time he took a breath. We could hardly believe that he was alive, but he was and continued to breathe, so we made hasty plans to evacuate him to the 67th Evacuation Hospital. We learned that he passed away within two hours of his arrival there.

The rest suffered shrapnel wounds of various degrees of seriousness; the worst was a fellow had lost a foot and had abdominal injuries. Another patient died on the operating table just as they finished surgery. And so it goes. From three in the morning to 7:30 AM I spent all my time in the Emergency Room starting intra-catheters for the administration of blood and I.V. fluids, taking vital signs, preparing patients for surgery and reassuring casualties. It is a big job and a very tiring one; I don't like to complain when I am dealing with such awful injuries, but my legs and feet do ache constantly from exhaustion, but it is very difficult to sleep during the day because of the heat and humidity.

Even so, I really can't feel anything but gratitude that I still have legs and feet that can ache.

Tuesday, 7 May, 1968: We had a party this evening for the five nurses who will be transferring to the 95th Evac Hospital at Danang. They are Eleanor Kutchoodon, Jeanne Guilbault, Pat Conlan, Dianne King and Lt.

Lutz. They leave on Thursday.

Wednesday, 8 May, 1968: It's a girl! My second delivery was done this morning at 6:25 AM, but it was the first baby for the mother. We got along well and there were no complications; the baby was large and healthy.

We also had a GI in surgery since 8:00 PM yesterday evening. Lots went wrong, and we had given him 24 units of blood.

Also, the dust-off pilots flew seven missions today and brought in two American D.O.A.s and several other severely wounded GIs. with gunshot wounds to the chest, neck, etc. There is apparently a lot of activity in the area where they were flying these missions and later, when I was trying to sleep, there was almost continuous noise from helicopters and ambulances pulling up to the Emergency Room and delivering casualties.

Saturday, 11 May, 1968: Spend the last three days very sick and they are pretty much lost to me, although I am feeling much better again today. Still, it is probably a blessing that I didn't get my R&R when I had originally requested it, since I wouldn't have felt much like going. Lost another GI this forenoon, the third one this week. Terrible wounds.

Sunday, 12 May, 1968: Mother's Day, 1968. God bless my mother and all other mothers who are sharing her anguish of separation this year because their sons are serving in this conflict in Southeast Asia.

I still don't feel very well; it seems like I just can't quite get my stomach to feeling right.

Fairly slow on the ward; we did received several Vietnamese with frag wounds, but they were immediately evacuated to Qui Nhon.

Wednesday, 15 May, 1968: Finally had a good, sound night's sleep and woke up feeling better for the first time in nearly two weeks.

Happy about that, but sadly, we lost a little Vietnamese boy at 2:00 AM from what we suspect was meningitis.

Saturday, 18 May, 1968: We received word today that the rest of the men from the 616th will be leaving soon; they were placed on 72 hour alert. This will leave us with only 17 corpsmen for the entire 100 bed hospital, and besides, we have had no replacements for the nurses that were transferred out. As a result, I will be starting 12 hour shifts seven days a week starting in the morning, making for an 84 hour week.

Sunday, 19 May, 1968: First of my twelve hour shifts. I am back in E.R., where I haven't been for a while. It was a quiet day, and a very, very hot one. Later I saw the movie *'Who's Afraid Of Virginia Woolf'.* Different!

Tuesday, 21 May, 1968: A sad day in the hospital: We lost three Vietnamese patients. The first was an older papasan who had burr holes drilled last night following a scooter accident. Then there was a small child whose problem we were unable to diagnose—he went into cardiac arrest in the emergency room, and then again on Ward #1. Finally, a premature baby born of a woman with carcinoma died.

A hard rain fell throughout the night.

Friday, 24 May, 1968: One more day closer to the beginning of my R&R (Rest and Relaxation) trip to Australia!

I slept until 6:15 AM in order to have enough time to get to the airport office at 0700 hrs.; from there I flew to Cam Ranh Bay aboard an 'Otter'—a small, single-engine plane that seats six passengers and seems to glide through the air. It was a clear and beautiful morning for flying. So beautiful was the expanse of countryside below that it made my heart ache to know what continuously goes on below.

The R&R processing office personnel instructed me to report back tomorrow with my luggage, dressed in a Class A khaki uniform.

I found a bunk in the air-conditioned officer's club where I ate supper, then spent my time writing letters and playing pinochle, then called it a day.

Saturday, 25 May, 1968: I have long awaited today and this incredible trip to Australia—eight hours by jet with a two-hour layover in Darwin for a plane check. Visiting Australia has truly been one of my life's dreams, even when I was a child in grade school studying world geography.

I sat in the shade until the officer's club opened, then wound up at a table for four along with two Warrant Officer pilots and a Special Forces captain. To someone who has not been in Vietnam, their stories would seem unbelievable. To me, they simply reaffirmed the things that I have been seeing during my time in-country: The results of war—scarred lives, mutilated bodies, damage, destruction and despair.

I so often wonder, 'Why?' in hope that one day, someone of courage and strength will find the answer.

Later in the afternoon, I exchanged my military payment certificates— 'funny money'—for honest to goodness 'greenbacks'. They looked so good they made me want to keep on going, straight back to the United States. Although, according to my calendar, that should happen in exactly 36 days!

The jet departed at 5:00 PM, and after the usual prayer for safety I usually say beforé take-off, we were mid-air above the South China Sea. Darkness soon overtook us, and at midnight, we landed in Darwin, where our immunization records were carefully scrutinized.

Sunday, 26 May, 1968: We departed Darwin for Sydney at 0200 hrs. This takes you across the entire continent, about 2000 miles, and thus, it took four hours. Landing was at precisely 0600 hrs. as no planes were allowed in the airport before that hour due to the noise.

The first thing that struck me was the tremendous temperature change: The thermometer read 54° F—a tremendous change from the nineties in Vietnam.

After our in-country briefing and money exchange from U.S. dollars to Australian currency, I took a room on the fifth floor of the Chevron-Hilton, a hotel that is completely glass-enclosed on one side, offering a spacious view of the Sydney Harbor Bay.

After a shower, I dressed to attend church services at the Wesley Methodist Chapel in downtown Sydney. This was quite an experience for me since I had not heard a church choir singing since departing the States. The minister was visiting from London and he delivered a fine message.

When the services ended, I window-shopped antique stores in the downtown area followed by a tasty and satisfying lunch of veal cordon bleu. This was two slices of pressed veal with layers of ham and Swiss cheese rolled and deep-fried.

I decided to walk back to the hotel, and even though the wind was brisk and the weather comparable to early November in the U.S., the sun shone brightly and warm.

Later, for dinner, I found a very nice restaurant called 'The Bourbon and Beef Steak', where I had a delicious meal of filet mignon served with an ample supply of broiled Australian lobster.

Monday, 27 May, 1968: I know this week will go by quickly, so I decided to make every minute count.

I spend the day browsing antique shops, first at Grafton Galleries, where I had been having running correspondence with the owner, Mr. Peter Cook, for quite a while and was disappointed to discover he had just left for a six month stay in England the week before. His assistant was very gracious and gave me the addresses of a few more shops that might be of interest; he also presented me with a copy of 'The Australian Antique

Collector'—a magazine edited by Mr. Cook. I found things very expensive at this shop, however, and throughout this area of town, I found them the same.

It was a beautiful morning for walking and I enjoyed taking my time, looking at the architecture of the houses and was pleased to see many fall flowers like chrysanthemums and poinsettias in full bloom.

I walked to Woollhara where I found many antique shops with prices more to my buying tastes. I bought some lovely items including cranberry glass, Mary Gregory glass, satin glass and colored hand lamps.

In the last shop of the day I had the greatest good fortune to meet a fellow named Ernest Elfingstone who overheard me asking the shopkeeper about some good old Wedgewood items. Ernest approached me and said that he thought he could help.

Sure enough, we took a taxi to the homes of some of his friends, and I ended up buying all the items they had for sale. This included a huge cheese dish with cover in the early soft brown color with classic figures all around it. I also purchased a brown teapot, also surrounded by classic figures. And a wine carafe with a stopper and a round dish that the carafe sits in. All items are of the vintage design and in perfect condition.

I returned to the hotel, got cleaned up and went to dinner at a French restaurant called Ozone II, where I was treated like royalty, served a delicious hot punch and enjoyed a meal of broiled lobster in wine sauce while seated before a roaring fire and entertained by a violinist playing soft music.

I then called it a day: It had been a wonderful and exciting one for me and I am anxious for tomorrow to begin!

Tuesday, 28 May, 1968: Another lovely day for antique shopping, and I really hit the jackpot. I bought the most beautiful item that I expect to find on my combined business and pleasure trip here: A small, decorated Burmese rose bowl on a ruffled pedestal. I am thrilled with it!

I also bought a large quantity of items from a woman with a shop in Valcluse; primarily art glass and a magnificent set of Havilland china.

I am so impressed with Sydney's cleanliness and how friendly the people can be, eager to help and interested in visitors to their city. I can certainly understand why it is such a popular R&R destination for American soldiers. I wish I could stay here longer.

Wednesday, 29 May, 1968: Today, I took a break from antique hunting and enjoyed an all-day tour of the city: We left the hotel at 9:00 AM and did not return until 6:00 PM. The tour was advertised as 'a hundred miles' around the city and I am sure that it was every bit of that.

Sydney is a huge city, and all the buildings are made of red clay tile, making it a most colorful and interesting picture from a hilltop, gazing over acre after acre of homes. In fact, points in the city are measured from the central post office, and it is nearly twenty miles in any direction before you reach the city limits. The boys and girls each go to separate schools and each wear uniforms, although many men wear Bermuda shorts to work! The women wear mini-skirts almost exclusively, and believe me, they are mighty mini!

Another interesting study is the food shops, as there are no supermarkets as we might think of them in the States. You would need to stop at three or more places to prepare a full meal, since one shop may handle canned goods, another frozen goods and still another fresh meat.

Ernest and I had dinner together this evening at the same place I dined last night, ending another full and busy day.

Thursday, 30 May, 1968: The packers came early to my hotel room to prepare my purchases for shipment by boat to the United States, and by the time they had finished they had 15 boxes! It should arrive in Norfolk, VA around the middle of August, and I shall be most anxious! It will be like Christmas in the middle of summer.

I took a tour of Australian 'bush' country today. After leaving the city, we drove into mountainous and rural areas, very scenic and beautiful. We had a picnic lunch of fried steak and cabbage salad, following which there was a boomerang exhibition. It is now a sport but was once used for killing game. We all got our chance at the art, although some of us did better than others!

After dinner we visited an animal sanctuary where we saw all of the famous Australian animals like kangaroos and koalas. We were allowed to enter the fenced-in area with the kangaroos and pet them as they fed. One of the most thrilling sights to me was a mother kangaroo with a little one poking his head out of her pouch, just like on a picture post card.

Today I also had the wonderful fortune of meeting a fine young fellow named Bill Torres who sat beside me at the noon meal. Our conversation led to what the two of us had been doing over the past few days in Sydney, and when I mentioned antique hunting, his ears really perked up! He expressed a great interest in them and in further conversation we learned that we had a great deal in common. He is a Medical Corps officer from Louisiana who has been in Vietnam since September, and intends to take up a three year residency in obstetrics once he finishes his "hitch with Uncle Sam". We spent most of the rest of the week together and both feel that it is a shame we didn't meet earlier.

Bill and I had a marvelous smorgasbord meal at a downtown German restaurant called 'The Weinkeller', then walked around downtown and window-shopped. We also made early morning plans to visit the city market along with Ernest.

Friday, 31 May, 1968: The final day of my wonderful trip to Australia began early as I headed over to King's Cross shopping center to pick up a few items I had promised folks back at the unit and some things I wanted to send home. I was lucky enough to find Ellen some lovely Australian woolen material, including a nice piece of woven white wool that should make a beautiful suit or dress.

Just past ten, Bill and I took a cab to Ernest's shop in a suburb called Paddington and the three of us went down to the commercial harbor where we were just in time for the eleven o'clock opening of Paddy's Market—an enormously large market open only on Fridays and Saturdays. They sell nearly anything you could imagine, live chickens, fresh flowers, second-hand merchandise, even tanned kangaroos hides—one of which I bought, along with several antiques.

From there, we walked to the midtown section and found some fairly exclusive downtown antique shops where I was fortunate enough to run across a lovely dark-blue Wedgewood pitcher.

From there we took a cab back to Ernest's shop where his mother had coffee and homemade passion fruit ice cream waiting for us; different from anything that Bill and I had ever experienced.

After bidding a fond farewell to Ernest and his mother, Bill and I returned to the hotel, and met again later for a final Sydney dinner at Ozone II—a special meal of roast pheasant, boiled new potatoes and French bread. Then we walked around the King's Cross section of town, which is similar to Greenwich Village in New York, but not so "way out".

It was then time to call it a day as we both had an early arising hour before departure.

Saturday, 1 June, 1968: After a series of busy days, that 6:00 alarm came way too quickly! After debriefing in the hotel ballroom, we headed to the airport and boarded a Pan American Jet Clipper and flew back to the place where I have spent eleven long months: Vietnam.

Sunday, 2 June, 1968: I returned to the unit just in time for the officer's brunch, held on the patio on the first Sunday of every month. I must admit, the surroundings were all too familiar.

I learned that the military had made a "push" the previous Saturday and had received a large number of casualties, losing several fellows even as they were being given medical treatment.

I probably should not say that I am glad that I missed it, but I am. I have seen way too much of that.

My roommate informed me that he had received his port call and would be leaving the unit to return home in the morning. Another officer who is scheduled to return home the same day as I said that he had learned through a telephone call to Qui Nhon that the two of us would be leaving around the 27th of June. What good news that was!

But with the good news, some bad. Among the 30 letters and tapes that were waiting for me was one from my folks informing me that my most dear friend and former nursing school roommate Jerry Baumgartner, had passed away the previous Tuesday morning. Although it was expected, it was still difficult to grasp as being true. I can only be grateful that his long suffering has finally come to an end.

Tuesday, 4 June, 1968: A hard rain fell all night and I had trouble sleeping, so I prepared sympathy cards for his wife and mother. It was a difficult task, but one that had to be done.

Wednesday, 5 June, 1968: We have just heard the tragic news about the attempted assassination of Robert F. Kennedy in California, and his condition does not sound good; how tragedy does repeat itself in that family.

The Assassination of Robert F. Kennedy

In the early morning hours of June 5, 1968, Robert F. Kennedy, frontrunner for the Presidential nomination of the Democratic Party, was passing through the kitchen of the Ambassador Hotel when he was shot in the head by Sirhan Sirhan, a 24-year-old Palestinian/Jordanian immigrant.

Minutes earlier, Kennedy had announced a major win in the California Democratic presidential primary.

Although Kennedy's wound was mortal, he survived for twenty-six hours in the nearby Good Samaritan Hospital.

His assassination had a major impact on the course of the Vietnam War. Had he lived, he had a reasonable shot at becoming the Democratic nominee—Hubert Humphrey was actually leading in delegates at the time of his death—although his election to the Presidency was far from a sure thing. These were still the days of the big 'Party Bosses' who considered Kennedy too young and radical to carry their interests into the future.

However, for the sake of speculation, had Kennedy been elected President, it is certain that his administration would have taken a far different course than that of Richard Nixon, who ultimately won the Presidential Elections of 1968.

Kennedy was absolutely sincere in his plan to extricate the United States from the 'quagmire' in Southeast Asia, and although his advisors—in particular, Averell Harriman—cautioned him against a policy of 'cut and run', Kennedy may or may not have taken this advice. What is clear is that the direction of a Robert Kennedy administration would have been first to make a negotiated settlement with North Vietnam, followed by a concerted focus on dealing with domestic racism and poverty.

Immediately following Kennedy's murder, it has been charged that Nixon—fearful that if Johnson's peace efforts in Vietnam began to payoff he would have a tougher time beating Hubert Humphrey in November—actually had a liaison approach South Vietnam President Nguyen van Thieu, to resist efforts to force him to the peace table.

In fact, when on October 31ˢᵗ, 1968, Johnson ordered a cease-fire in order to urge the NVA and the Vietcong to peace talks, Thieu announced that his government would not take place in the negotiations. And, less than a week later, with a one-point margin in the popular vote, Nixon was elected President.

If this version of events is correct, it means that Richard Nixon may have been directly responsible for the deaths of 20,000 more Americans in Vietnam before a final settlement was reached seven years later.

Thursday, 6 June, 1968: The news arrived at around 1700 hrs. that Robert F. Kennedy has died. I feel so sorry for his family, especially his parents, who look so old and tired, having to go through another tragedy. The saying that "money can't buy happiness" is brought home to us once again, and never more clearly.

Sunday, 9 June, 1968: I had a terrible time staying awake at work, but at the end, when I left, there was a most beautiful sunrise. Rays of red beamed out from behind the mountain and across the valley to the east, giving it the appearance of a gigantic crown studded with amber and ruby jewels.

Tuesday, 11 June, 1968: Today is the day that I have awaited for almost a year: I received my port call and will be leaving Vietnam at midnight on June 28, 1968. Seventeen days away.

My hold luggage left today and boy, does my room look empty!

Wednesday, 12 June, 1968: I could hardly believe how quiet it was tonight, both in the hospital and outside the post. I barely heard a shot fired. In the morning we evacuated about 25 patients to Qui Nhon and if we don't get any more in during the night, our census will be very low.

Thursday, 13 June 1968: More activity today, beginning with a young GI who was dead on arrival, killed in action while on patrol with his platoon, suffering a gunshot wound to the face. He was accompanied by his buddy, who was suffering severe and debilitating shock. Then in the afternoon we received twenty Vietnamese CIDGs (Civilian Irregular Defense Group) whose bus had struck a land mine. About eleven required admittance.

The remainder of the 616th received word today that they should be prepared to move out at any time—the third or fourth such alerts they have received. That would leave only ten corpsmen for the entire hospital. Thus, we are back to seven-day weeks, twelve hours per day.

Friday, 14 June, 1968: A busy night, mostly spent caring for the casualties received yesterday, and in part because we had some new corpsmen unfamiliar with the night duty routine.

Monday, 17 June, 1968: The compound received mortar fire tonight for the first time in many weeks. They sounded extremely close, inside the perimeter, but we only received three patients as a result, and these were for observation only. We did manage to get all the patients into the bunker in a very short period of time, and I'm grateful for that.

Tuesday, 19 June, 1968: Ten more days and I am homeward bound!

We had another mortar attack last night, beginning at around 9:15 PM, which is relatively early, especially since it was a very clear, starlit night.

Thursday, 20 June, 1968: This letter is being written from the 12th Air Force Hospital at Cam Ranh Bay where I will work tonight and then tomorrow night, which will be my last night of duty as well as my 17th straight day of working without a day off.

I am about at my wit's end and ready to wrap it up.

Thursday, 22 June, 1968: What a send-off for my last night of work! It was one of the busiest nights I can recall. I really doubt I can find the time to finish this account of it, but God willing, I can squeeze it in over the next few minutes.

It is now 2:30 AM and I have been on duty since 7:00 PM last evening; we have been receiving casualties steadily so that now, 75 of our 80 beds are filled.

At 7:20 PM, a Vietnamese woman expired after having been hospitalized for around 24 hours; she had been convulsing since being admitted yesterday, and I did not think she would survive that shift, but she did not die until shortly after I came on duty tonight. After we had taken care of those details, we received a patient with cellulitis of the hand, and then two patients from O.R. with chest tubes who needed to be watched closely. Also, three Vietnamese civilians who have had surgery in the past two days to repair perforated lower intestines caused by typhoid—they also require extensive care due to the fluids they are receiving and nasogastric tubes, suction, etc.

At 8:00 PM we received a Vietnamese woman who was about to go into labor; the doctor told us that he might not be able to get to her in time, and not to be surprised if I wound up with another delivery on my record. The problem is that this is the woman's 17th pregnancy, and she had lost 14 of her previous babies. The doctor wanted me to know what I might be facing.

At 10:30, a patient arrived at the emergency room with stab wounds in the arm from a fight he'd been involved in at an enlisted men's club; he had severed brachial artery and had to be taken to the operating room immediately. He had lost a considerable amount of blood and looked terrible—we discovered that the weapon used on him was a machete.

To top all that off, I have come down with a very painful ear infection. It has been so long since I had one that I barely remembered what they felt like. It is now three in the morning, which means that I have only four more hours to work before finishing up for good.

Letter interrupted for an important announcement!

At 3:30 AM yours truly delivered a live, healthy baby girl to the Vietnamese woman. Mother and baby (and 'boxie': Vietnamese for 'doctor') are doing very well. I am proud and pleased! Now, Miss Florence Wilson in Quincy, Illinois, what do you think of that?! I have delivered three healthy babies this year. Do you think before long I will qualify for that midwife certificate?

Sunday, June 23, 1968: It is now midnight, and what a beautiful, still evening it is. My intention of going to church this morning were foiled due to a faulty alarm clock—I ended up sleeping until high noon. I am just finishing up writing farewell letters to some of the folks who have been helpful to me on the night shift these past few weeks.

Monday, June 24, 1968: Today's activities included a trip to finance to pick up my advance travel pay—$163—and to secure the ten days travel time I will need between Ft. Lewis, Washington and Ft. Belvoir, Virginia. I said goodbye to the P-X with a final trip to pick up some necessary travel supplies.

At 3:30 PM, my fellow officers held a farewell get-together for me in the mess hall where I was presented with a nice plaque and going-away card. In the evening, we had yet another party at the Hong Kong East officer's club, this time with steak!

Meanwhile, the war goes on: Some MIKE forces were brought in this afternoon from contact with NVA about 25 miles away.

Wednesday, 26 June, 1968: The red-letter day I have so long awaited: Today, I leave for Cam Ranh Bay, and then home. Even so, I didn't sleep well last night: There was a lot of firing on the green line, and boy, as such a short timer, did it ever make me nervous!

Conclusion: The Vietnam War, Protests to Peace: The Nixon Era

Richard Nixon settled into the Oval Office with twin objectives regarding Vietnam. His obliquely stated intention was to end the war on his own terms during his first year in office, and in the meantime, he pushed his law-and-order platform by coming down hard on anti-war demonstrators. The infamous Kent State shootings on Monday, May 4, 1970, when four, unarmed students at a campus demonstration were killed by the Ohio National Guard, occurred at the mid-way point of Nixon's first term in office.

Nixon can be credited for encouraging the POW-MIA movement, concerned about the treatment of the known prisoners of war (POWs) in captivity in North Vietnam, and equally, with the whereabouts of those classified as missing in action (MIA). Throughout the remainder of his first term, he continued to work toward a peace settlement that would be satisfactory to Americans, doubtlessly concerned that 'peace without honor' would affect the outcome of the 1972 election.

One week before that election, Henry Kissinger—Nixon's national security adviser—announced that a peace accord had been reached with North Vietnam, but failed to mention that South Vietnam had refused to accept the negotiated terms. Nixon won a landslide victory.

The peace talks in Paris finally succeeded in producing a cease-fire agreement on January 27, 1973, and the last U.S. troops left Vietnam on March 29, 1973. It was understood by both the President and his advisers as well as the Saigon government that South Vietnam would not be able to resist a major communist attack. And in fact, In early 1975, North Vietnam made another big push and toppled the South Vietnamese government. South Vietnam officially surrendered to communist North Vietnam on April 30, 1975.

On July 2, 1976, Vietnam was reunited as a communist country, the Socialist Republic of Vietnam, which it remains today.

According to the Department of Defense, the direct cost of the Vietnam

War was $173 billion. Potential veterans' benefits of $220 billion, with $31 billion must be added to that figure. Of course, veterans received educational benefits, enhancing research and design in certain fields. It can't be denied that expenditures in the defense industry provided jobs for millions that might not have been there in otherwise.

The War in Vietnam was considered 'limited' in the sense that all available offensive options—including the use of tactical nuclear weapons—were not deployed. Nonetheless, the conflict had a profound impact on all areas of American life; social, political, economic, and strategic, and the fallout from this impact affects our culture to this day.

AFTERWORD

Fred Phelps remained in the Army Nurse Corps for 22 ½ years following his tour of duty in Vietnam, criss-crossing the country in numerous assignments at various military hospitals. He retired in April, 1989, having been promoted to the rank of Colonel.

Following retirement, he spent several years working as a staff nurse in medical/surgical units at small, local hospitals around his hometown of Colesburg, Iowa, where he lives today with Ellen. They have been married for 50 years.

He continues to indulge his passion, antiques, and runs a successful business called 'Landmark Antiques' in Colesburg. Glass is his particular love, and he is a member and past president of several national glass collecting organizations.

Fred continues to express his loyalty and community commitment by serving as a hospice volunteer while serving on many church, county, and community boards and committees.

There are no 'typical' Vietnam veterans, but it is fair to suggest that Fred Phelps has taken the trauma of having served in one of the most violent and uncertain periods of that conflict and transformed the experience into something positive. For that, we can all add an additional note of thanks to him for his service, both during wartime and during peace.

Fred and Ellen Phelps, 2012

18782269R00066

Made in the USA
Charleston, SC
20 April 2013